THE TENSAW RIVER

T0274256

THE TENSAW RIVER

Alabama
THE FORGE OF HISTORY

A SERIES OF ILLUSTRATED GUIDES

Alabama's Hidden Heritage Corridor

MIKE BUNN

THE UNIVERSITY OF ALABAMA PRESS *Tuscaloosa*

The University of Alabama Press
Tuscaloosa, Alabama 35487-0380
uapress.ua.edu

Inquiries about reproducing material from this work should
be addressed to the University of Alabama Press.

Typeface: Arno Pro

Cover images: *Top*, Historic Blakeley State Park on the Tensaw River in
Alabama, Carol M. Highsmith, photographer, The George F. Landegger
Collection of Alabama Photographs in Carol M. Highsmith's America,
Library of Congress, Prints and Photographs Division; *bottom*, Autumn
on the Tensaw, photograph courtesy of Sherry Stimpson Frost
Cover design: Lori Lynch

Publication of *The Tensaw Delta* is generously supported by the
University of Alabama Center for Economic Development.

Cataloging-in-Publication data is available from the Library of Congress.
ISBN: 978-0-8173-6172-3 (paper)
E-ISBN: 978-0-8173-9532-2

For Tonya, my partner on the journey

Contents

CONTENTS

Acknowledgments

BOOK PROJECTS SUCH AS THIS ONE ARE ALWAYS A GROUP EF-fort. I am especially indebted to all of those who have helped me refine this manuscript in its various stages of development, including Joel Borden, Ian Brown, and especially my colleagues and friends Greg Waselkov and John Sledge. Their constructive criticism has helped me improve many parts of this book and avoid missteps so that the narrative is clearer and stronger. Any shortcomings that remain in spite of their expert review are of course my own.

Numerous other people provided assistance to me as this project took shape. Bob Peck, the ever-generous volunteer keeper of the Historic Mobile Preservation Society Archives, conducted a thorough search for information that might be useful. Sherry Stimpson Frost volunteered herself to ride along on multiple Historic Blakeley State Park cruises so that she could photograph the Tensaw River from its upper reaches to where it meets the bay. Kristina Pittman, director of the North Baldwin Chamber of Commerce, graciously allowed me the use of some of the images of the Tensaw the chamber had in its files. My friends Kathy Hicks, Brody

Joe Thommasen, and Brian Kelso likewise kindly made available their stunning photography of scenes along the remarkable waterway. Jada Jones at the Doy Leale McCall Rare Book and Manuscript Library at the University of South Alabama searched through her institution's robust collections for images that would enhance the story I attempt to tell here. The staffs of all the local libraries, especially the Daphne Public Library, Fairhope Public Library, and Foley Public Library, were, as usual, gracious and extraordinarily helpful.

Above all I want to thank the people and institutions who believed in this project and supported it when, for a variety of reasons, it might have been turned down. This includes its generous financial supporters, my friend Judge Tim Russell, and the University of Alabama Center for Economic Development, whose assistance was instrumental in bringing it to publication. Finally, I owe a special note of thanks to Dan Waterman and all of those at the University of Alabama Press for helping transform this book from concept to reality. I can only hope that all those who were a part of its production are as proud of it as I am.

THE TENSAW RIVER

Introduction

R IVERS ENCOURAGE REFLECTION. WHETHER WATCHING the peaceful flow of a river as it rolls by or on a journey afloat on one's waters, pondering the experience of times past comes easy streamside. In my work as director of Historic Blakeley State Park in Baldwin County, Alabama, I have been allowed the privilege of frequently traversing the course of one of Alabama's most historic yet unheralded rivers as I guided tours exploring its wealth of human history and aided visitors in discovery of its outstanding natural environment. That river, the forty-one-mile-long Tensaw, forms the eastern boundary of the natural wonder that is the Mobile-Tensaw Delta as it traverses through a relatively little-developed region whose cultural identity is in many ways characterized more by what was than what is. It is a forgotten but important heritage corridor. The river manifests a quiet physical grandeur made all the more poignant by a rich human past, but understanding the interplay of both those heritages requires knowledge of their existence—awareness that quite frankly is not common at least in part due to a rather thin historiographical record. It is my hope that this book will serve as an introduction to the rich and legendary natural and cultural heritage of one of Alabama's most overlooked but significant waterways.

Most of the more celebrated stories associated with the Delta area are connected directly with the Mobile River, the watery western boundary of the region and home to the venerable city with which it shares a name. In comparison to its sister river, though, the Tensaw stands unsung, a bit of an unknown quantity on the

Aerial view of the Tensaw from Historic Blakeley State Park. Photograph by Brian Kelso, courtesy of Historic Blakeley State Park.

landscape of Alabama's historical literature. The reasons are many. For starters, there is no major urban entity similar to Mobile extant along its banks, which, in addition to serving as a major population center, once figured prominently in military campaigns. There are no major industrial establishments on its course, nor is it a heavily trafficked commercial thoroughfare, and it has no harbor in which oceangoing ships from international ports currently dock. Yet this has not always been so. Therein lies the river's enduring allure to those interested in the past, for it has borne witness to former glories, trials, and dramas every bit as compelling as those found on

Autumn on the Tensaw. Courtesy of Sherry Stimpson Frost.

any of the state's other riverways. The incongruity of past activity and present calm becomes particularly powerful along the Tensaw once one becomes aware of the scope and scale of its amazing past.

This book is a sort of historical travelogue of the Tensaw River, exploring the turns and bends of its course over time in an effort to introduce readers to its remarkable story. It is not a traditional chronological history of the river, nor does it give equal weight or space to particular eras or geographic sections. Rather, it is an introduction to what I think are the river's most salient and unique

human dramas, all introduced by an expression of its matchless natural setting and concluded with an honest assessment of its current state and future prospects.

I do not profess to have any special knowledge greater than that of others who have written about and investigated the region's past, and I am especially a novice in interpreting the rich natural diversity found along the Tensaw's banks. The river and its story have entranced me, though, capturing my imagination with their larger-than-life physical scale and the enduring importance of the special cultural history that played out on and alongside the stream's murky waters. I believe that communicating this historical essence in narrative form will stir the imagination of others, as well. Alabama is blessed with more than its fair share of amazing cultural and natural heritage landscapes, but few are as visually so close in appearance to what they once were as the Tensaw watershed. It contains an uncommon wealth of history and a bountiful environment that begs for definition and rediscovery.

This book's format is inspired in large part by some of the unconventional classics of Alabama literature I have come to know and love, each for different reasons—Helen P. Akens and Virginia P. Brown's *Alabama: Mounds to Missiles*; Virginia Van der Veer Hamilton's *Alabama: A History*; Harvey Jackson's *Inside Alabama*; Sue Walker's *In the Realm of Rivers: Alabama's Mobile-Tensaw Delta*; and Valerie Pope Burns and Robin McDonald's *Visions of the Black Belt: A Cultural Survey of the Heart of Alabama*, to name a few. These books, published in different eras over the course of several decades and admittedly involving varying levels of scholarship and for different purposes, nonetheless share some commonalities that have inspired the creation of this narrative. They are each in some way celebratory of an extravagant past that defines a particular region, and either overtly or subtly seek in different ways to communicate the essence of a complicated identity-forming heritage worthy of remembrance. They are set in real places and involve real people who performed real deeds and endured real trials. Akens and Brown take a storytelling approach to their narrative, presenting state history in a series of vignettes through time, while Jackson and Hamilton take a conversational, topical approach to explaining equally troubling and noteworthy historical trends in Alabama history in laymen's terms. The work of Walker, Burns, and McDonald is more of a multi-discipline, multisensory documentary approach to comprehending different unique natural and cultural environments in mind, body, and spirit. I admit to not having done precisely what any of these esteemed authors have done in their distinguished works, but their style and purpose have nonetheless inspired this creation. I must confess that perhaps the most direct influence on my approach to this work, however, is John Sledge's masterful, scholarly yet relaxed, account of the Mobile River (*The Mobile River*). In that volume the author presents with a storyteller's flare a definitive account of the history of a river that has figured large indeed in Alabama's rich past. That book made me wonder if the Mobile's sister stream might not merit having its own story told in some fashion. A collective regional identity for the greater Mobile-Tensaw region has been rather slow in coming into its own, after all, and there is certainly room for additional literature on the region's remarkable and distinct heritage.

The Tensaw River is a place richly deserving of celebration. In the pages that follow it is my goal to acquaint readers with some of the most important parts of its abundant natural and cultural heritage so that it stands more distinct and visible in our consciousness. Place and heritage are inherently closely intertwined concepts in the human experience, and it is high time the mighty Tensaw River be recognized for its distinction on both those counts. I invite you to come along, then, on a virtual journey of discovery along this ancient and storied stream.

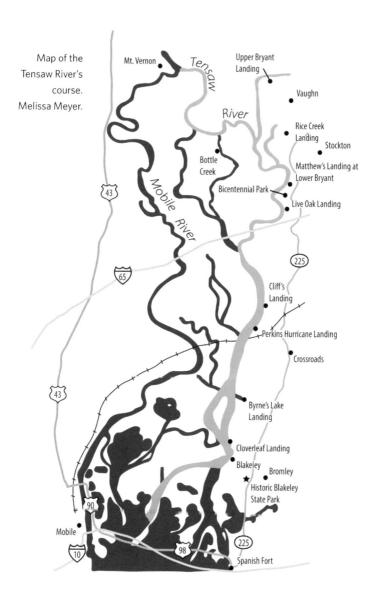

Map of the Tensaw River's course. Melissa Meyer.

Mt. Vernon

Tensaw River

Upper Bryant Landing

Vaughn

Rice Creek Landing

Stockton

Bottle Creek

Matthew's Landing at Lower Bryant

Bicentennial Park

Live Oak Landing

Mobile River

Cliff's Landing

Perkins Hurricane Landing

Crossroads

Byrne's Lake Landing

Cloverleaf Landing

Blakeley

Bromley

Historic Blakeley State Park

Mobile

Spanish Fort

1

~~~~

Primeval Waterway

THE TENSAW RIVER'S HISTORY IS MEASURED IN EONS AND involves irresistible forces that have shaped the land through which it flows for thousands of years. Volcanoes, earthquakes, ice ages, and the inundation and recession of primordial seas have all played their role over the centuries in bringing about the venerable waterway as it exists today. Any understanding of the Tensaw must start with an appreciation of that timeless essence.

It adds something to our grasp of the river in its physical reality to know that millions of years of geologic history have influenced the path it takes today. Scientists tell us the region through which it flows was formed along a fault line in the planet's continental crust created by the meeting of tectonic plates during the breakup of the super continent Pangaea around 180 million years ago. Epochal fluctuations in sea levels, largely due to the advance and retreat of hemisphere-altering glaciation, resulted in the Delta, and much of the southern half of Alabama, periodically being under sea in ancient times. In others, the coastline extended far into the present gulf. The preserved remnants of antediluvian forests yet standing but submerged dozens of miles off the Alabama coast

The Tensaw at Matthew's Lower Bryant Landing. Courtesy of Mike Bunn.

bear silent witness to this ebb and flow that has taken place on a scale and a timeline most of us can scarcely comprehend. Over the ages the location of Mobile Bay and head of the river system that feeds it has actually moved north and south on several occasions. The Mobile-Tensaw Delta, the wetlands through which the Tensaw and its sister river, the Mobile, flow, has existed in its current location for less than 10,000 years—the geologic blink of an eye, but an eternity to us in the twenty-first century.

A national natural landmark known by some as "America's Amazon," the Delta is formed by the meeting of many waters. It is a massive region of wetlands over forty-five miles long and on average about fifteen miles wide. It is the second largest delta in the country—only the Mississippi River delta is larger—and the

mouth of a river system discharging the fourth largest volume of water to a coastal area anywhere in North America. The Delta features approximately 200,000 acres of some of the least disturbed natural environments in all of the southeastern United States. It contains more than 20,000 acres of open water, including rivers, creeks, bayous, and lakes, as well as over 80,000 acres of marshes and swamps, and at least another 85,000 acres of bottomland forest. The Delta, technically in geological terms a drowned alluvial plain, empties on average some 62,100 cubic feet of water per second into Mobile Bay every day. The rivers that flow into it drain a large swath of the American southeast and account for an estimated 14 percent of all freshwater flows in the continental United States. Tumbling into this aquatic wonder are the combined drainages of the Alabama and Tombigbee River systems; numerous large streams and rivulets winding their way toward the Gulf of Mexico from the northeast Mississippi foothills and the mountainous reaches of western Georgia and southeastern Tennessee, down through the rolling prairies of central Alabama, and effortlessly funneling themselves ever-closer together as they lazily cut their channels across the coastal plain. The entire interconnected river system is known as the Mobile River Basin. Approximately 44,000 square miles in area, it ranks as the sixth largest basin in the United States.

The Alabama and the Tombigbee join at a junction forming the southernmost boundary of Clarke County, Alabama. Thence, as one stream these venerable rivers flow together briefly as the deep, wide, and roiling Mobile River until, just a few miles south of the site of Fort Stoddert, the Mobile itself branches into two separate streams. On the west, the Mobile continues on toward its namesake city, its dark waters figuratively leaving a wake of history as they wash ashore through the gloaming wilderness of the Delta, down through the industrial activity of the busy port of Mobile, and past Alabama's oldest city as it empties into the glistening waters of Mobile Bay. The eastern branch is the Tensaw. From its division from the Mobile (approximate GPS waypoint: 31.06795°N 87.96306°W), it travels some forty-one twisting miles on the way to the bay, its course describing the eastern boundary of the Mobile-Tensaw Delta. Off its main channel branches the Middle River, Mifflin Lake, and the waters of a sprawling estuary known simply as The Basin, all former paths of the Tensaw. Depths vary from spots of less than ten feet to holes up to 100 feet along the river's course, and it alternates in width from just over 100 feet to several hundred yards as its brown waters make their way southward.

Life abounds along the Tensaw. The river and the larger Delta are home to an astonishingly diverse biological scene made possible by the confluence of geography and climate. The only temperate region in the world with similar biodiversity is found in Southeast Asia. A canopy of tree species that ranks as among the most diverse in all of North America shades a landscape with a teeming proliferation of flora and fauna. The stately bald cypress, some individual specimens thriving for centuries, are the monarchs of this vast forest, their girth and height occasionally reaching astounding proportions. Most of the best examples of these grand trees were cut down by loggers long ago, but the few giants that remain standing in the marshy soil strike one with awe at what once was in this landscape . . . and what might yet be again. They stand as some of the few subtle reminders that this landscape has been altered by man, after all. A one-time state champion bald cypress in Alabama, for many years the largest recorded type of its species in the state, stands just off of Bayou Jessamine, one of the many small creeks connecting to the Tensaw's main channel. With a trunk measuring over twenty-seven feet in circumference, the tree is easily distinguishable among its peers and stretches skyward with impressive reach despite the fact its top was damaged by a storm at some point in the distant past. It is centuries old, how many is anyone's guess, but the lowest estimates place it at about 300 years of age. Some claim it is much, much older, perhaps a millennium or more. But things grow fast in the warm, wet, subtropical environment of the Delta, and it may be easier to imagine this stately tree

Pelican in flight over the Tensaw. Photography by Dragon Fly Photography, courtesy of the North Baldwin Chamber of Commerce.

bearing witness to scenes measured by the scores of decades than the even more impressive realization that it is a part of one of the most lush growing environments on the continent and might have reached its staggering dimensions much quicker than supposed.

But the cypress is just one part of a plethora of species found in an area that is home to one of the highest diversity of trees anywhere in North America. Cottonwood, hickory, elm, maple, sycamore, ash, hop hornbeam, sweetgum, and several types of oaks are just a few of the many species that shade the upper and middle Tensaw's shores and the hinterland filled with creeks, bayous, and rivulets feeding into it. Beneath their canopy grow enormous, trackless stands of the ubiquitous bluestem palm, their fan-shaped leaves seemingly an endless maze of monotonous evergreen growth than can be tricky to navigate even for short distances as they obscure landmarks and dampen sound. Bountiful rainfall combined with a warm climate and a rich alluvial soil enriched by deposits from yearly flooding yields an astonishing variety of woody stemmed and herbaceous flowers, shrubs, and grasses growing on, under, and all around these most visible species for much of the venerable river's course. Along the river's southern reaches as it approaches Mobile Bay and the firm high ground gives way to low-slung swampy banks, fewer trees are found and the landscape becomes

Alligator on the Tensaw. Courtesy of Kathy Hicks.

one of open marshes, thick submerged grassbeds, and expansive groves of waterborne lilies.

Throughout these environments can be found a diverse assemblage of animals all relying to varying degrees on the river's life-giving waters. Dozens of varieties of mollusks, more than eighty species of crustaceans, numerous amphibians and reptiles—including the greatest diversity of turtles on the planet—call the Delta region home. Some 184 types of fish, over 200 species of birds including regal bald eagles and ospreys, and more than 800 species of insects have been recorded in the region to date, and the count continues. Over fifty types of mammals are found along the Tensaw watershed, including virtually all of Alabama's most common

Lotus flowers in bloom. Courtesy of Kathy Hicks.

Dragonfly. Courtesy of Brody Joe Thommasen.

woodland creatures and, notably, one of its few populations of black bear. Occasionally there are unconfirmed reports of cougars roaming in the remotest reaches of the Delta, but the last documented evidence of them anywhere in the state occurred back in the 1950s. Like the buffalo that once roamed these wild expanses, they appear to be long gone, proof that even the wildest tracts of the state have not escaped the effects of human activity. That we sometimes persist in believing they, along with several other exotic species both extirpated and fanciful, might yet find a home in the Delta hints at our perception of it as one of Alabama's last truly wild places.

But statistics and summaries of its wildlife are inadequate to describe the Delta, both wellspring and progeny of the Tensaw. One must be afloat on the river's gently rolling waters or hear the lapping of the waves along its shores to be reminded of its antiquity. One must hear the squawk of the startled heron or the plunk of a turtle jumping into the brown water from a log perch to realize its wildness. At every turn along its course, one is reminded that this is a place apart, vibrating to rhythms thousands of years old that seem unaffected by the fast pace of modern life all around it, an island of relatively—at least in comparison with some other regional streams—unspoiled natural habitat adjacent to one of the fastest-growing corridors of development along the northern Gulf Coast.

In an era in which people are wont to rediscover and venerate nature, we sometimes conflate the terms *unspoiled* and *idyllic*. From the perspective of a twenty-first-century person, the harsh truth is that the Tensaw and its hinterlands are sometimes rather the opposite of a wonderland, at least for our species. The place is viscerally real and uncompromising, and for every aspect of its enchantment as an untamed natural environment are immediate reminders that it is an inconvenient and often uncomfortable place for humans to stay very long. The Delta contains swarms of biting insects such as annoying mosquitoes and stealthy ticks that, even in on a warm winter day, manifest themselves in alarming numbers. Visitors must be on guard for water moccasins lurking in one's path when traversing the landscape or crossing its streams for most months of the year, and insufferable humidity in this steamy waterworld can easily distract one from its wonder in spring, summer, and sometimes even early fall. Rainstorms are common to ubiquitous in the warmer months; the region in which the Tensaw cuts its path is among the wettest in North America, receiving average annual rainfall amounting to over sixty inches. Flooding in this lowland basin where the waters of multiple large river systems meet is a regular occurrence, the question being not so much *if* but for *how long* the high waters will prohibit access to certain areas. In certain periods of inundation, the entire region manifests itself as one large body of water from the eastern shores of the Tensaw to the western banks of the Mobile. On cool winter days it can seem temporarily paradisiacal, but the great majority of the time exploring the wilderness that bounds the Tensaw requires preparation, patience, and persistence. The Tensaw region is not casually visited and especially not effortlessly lived in; just ask anyone living on one of the houseboats along the river's stream at places such as Lower Bryant's Landing about dealing with regular and sustained high waters.

To experience the river requires a purposeful effort, but few would disagree that it is worth the while. The Tensaw's beauty, tranquility, and the sensation of remoteness it inspires can all be in their own way rewarding. The lack of easy accessibility only serves to make it more exotic, a place apart from our daily grind in the cookie-cutter subdivisions and strip malls where we spend most of our time. Its proximity to a major metropolitan area and some of the region's largest tourist destinations only strengthen the appeal. As noted naturalist E. O. Wilson has observed, the Delta through which the Tensaw courses "might just be the easiest natural land in the United States in which to get lost" even though it is located adjacent to a thriving metropolitan area along some of the most well-used travel corridors in the region.[1]

The middle reaches of the Tensaw near Gravine Island.
Courtesy of Mike Bunn.

Everywhere along the river's course are reminders of its antiquity and nature's terrible, inexorable, power. Numerous oxbows, or channels the river once traversed at some point in the distant past, beg entry as one ventures along the Tensaw's storied waters. Often referred to locally and on regional maps as lakes, some of these appear at their mouths to be as big as the river itself. These old river routes demonstrate vividly the ever-changing nature of the waterway and how frequently it alters its course over and through the silty, easily eroded, alluvial soil through which it flows. Among the sweeping turns and gentle bends that define the main channel in the river's northern reaches is an unusual hairpin curve that provides a stunning glimpse into this natural process. It is known by the ominous-sounding name of Devil's Bend, possibly in reference to the difficulty nineteenth-century steamboats encountered in maneuvering the sharp turn. As one descends the river, the channel sweeps slowly eastward before taking an abrupt turn almost due north and then plunging nearly due south. The spot shows up on even the oldest maps of the Delta region dating to the 1700s. One can easily appreciate the natural forces at work here and literally see an oxbow being formed at Devil's Bend. The spit of land dividing the river from itself is, at its narrowest point, mere yards of dark loamy soil on which a few trees and a smattering of palmettoes have taken root. In the blink of an eye, geologically speaking, the river will cut through this narrow barrier, leaving the infamous bend a dead lake.

Just south of Interstate 65, which cuts through the Delta on a series of bridges hurtling traffic to and from Mobile and central Alabama and beyond, the Tensaw gradually broadens out into a wider, grander body of water. Graceful, bay-like vistas prevail in favorable weather, while the brisk northern winds of Gulf Coast winters and the thunderstorms of summer turn this stretch of the river into a rolling, whitecapping, inland sea. The river's sheer scale seems to double as its western and eastern shorelines grow more distant. Between the interstate and Gravine Island—a local landmark that demarcates the entrance to a man-made ship channel formed decades ago—the river's route is more directly southward than in its upper reaches. A gentle and wide bend toward the east opens into an expanse of water a mile wide at Gravine. The rippling waters give it the appearance of a lake as much as a river, and

Aerial view of the Tensaw near Historic Blakeley State Park. Photograph by SkyBama, courtesy of Historic Blakeley State Park.

the low wailing of the wind over the open space is continual. A little farther on, just between Cloverleaf Landing and Historic Blakeley State Park, the river crashes into the last of the high riverside bluffs on which so much human history of the riverway has unfolded. The bluff itself is actively eroding, exposing layers of ancient sediment and remnants of twentieth-century development that remind one again of the shaping force the river remains even today. Below the bluff millions of gallons of water thrash and roll, carving out a hole known as one of the deepest spots in the entire Delta. Even in periods of low water, the muddy bottom of the river here lies over ninety feet below the water's surface. In time of flood, it is measured in triple digits.

On the river flows from there, sweeping past Historic Blakeley State Park and then taking a southwesterly tack as it glides toward

Mobile Bay. The Tensaw is deep and wide at Blakeley, figuratively matching the rich cultural legacy found on its eastern shore in one of the state's largest and most unique cultural and natural heritage attractions. The city of Mobile rises above the marsh in the distance opposite Blakeley, its modern skyscrapers the first visible sign of the metropolis that traces its roots back over some three storied centuries and the locus of much of life in the broader region today. Slicing through a wild and scenic swampland that seems a world removed from the bustle of the northern Gulf Coast's second largest city just two or three miles distant, the Tensaw drifts past Delvan Bay on the right and Chacoloochee Bay on the left before emptying

Mouth of the Tensaw River at Mobile Bay. Courtesy of Mike Bunn.

its waters into Mobile Bay in front of the venerable USS *Alabama*, the celebrated World War II battleship that helped America win the war in the Pacific so many decades past. Under the steady rumble of the traffic on the bridges of the Interstate 10 Bayway and the Mobile Causeway, the river's muddy waters mingle with the lapping waves of the bay as the horizon opens to an expanse of water stretching as far south as the eye can see.

2

<hr>

The Place Where the Gods Are

I F THE TENSAW ITSELF CAN BE SAID TO BE ANCIENT, ITS HU-
man habitation is only slightly less so. People have called the
river home and sustained themselves on its resources for thousands of years. In the process, the Tensaw's residents have imbued
it with a cultural heritage as deep, diverse, and remarkable as any of
its natural features.

We do not know precisely when the first humans ventured
into the Tensaw region, but people were certainly there, or at least
visiting with some regularity, thousands of years in the past. The
earliest Native Americans to tap into the rich resources of the
Tensaw probably did so as many as 10,000 years ago or more.
The relatively sparse archaeological record on the Archaic period
(ca. 8,000–1,000 BC) peoples, who lived seminomadic lifestyles
as they roamed in seasonal cycles through the landscape in pursuit
of game and wild foods, leaves this earliest chapter in the human
history of the region somewhat vague. Archaeologists have found
enough scattered evidence of temporary prehistoric settlements—
in the form of shell middens, stone tools, and trade goods originat-
ing far from the Tensaw's shores—to know that people were calling

the area home for extended periods of time as early as 5,000 years ago. As compared to later eras, though, the artifactual evidence is frustratingly sparse. Perhaps deep beneath the dark layers of silty soil deposited by millennia of flooding in the wetlands through which the Tensaw cuts its course yet lie caches of items that may help complete the story of this formative period in regional human history. For now, we have to rely on informed inference in attempting to understand these first Delta peoples. That supposition tells us the Delta's original residents likely lived much as people of their era elsewhere lived. Perhaps they just ate a bit more fish and shellfish.

Our knowledge about later eras of human history in the Delta region subsequent to those first arrivals is greater, specifically as it pertains to the people of the Woodland period (1000 BC–AD 1000). The archaeological record on these inhabitants is much more substantial and informs us of fundamental differences between their lives and the lives of those who came before them. The people of the Woodland period along the Tensaw spent their days as a part of larger communities than had their ancestors; they stayed longer in one place than had those forebears; relied on sophisticated trade networks covering large swaths of the eastern half of the continent; participated in more elaborate spiritual rituals and burial practices; developed progressively more refined tools with which they hunted, farmed, fished, and built their homes. Perhaps most important of all, they mastered the art of transforming clay into pottery using water, fire, and ample amounts of skill. Pottery revolutionized their lifestyles, enabling new ways of storing and cooking food and providing an outlet for artistic expression as they

Bottle Creek. Courtesy of Sherry Stimpson Frost.

displayed utilitarian aptitude. In fact, to understand the designs they used in decorating and forming their bowls, pots, and jars is to be able at times to pinpoint the place and time in which they were created. Fragments of these vessels can be found throughout the region in which the Tensaw flows, tangible testimony to long-lost communities. The most visible reminders of the presence of the Woodland peoples, however, are the numerous large shell middens they left behind. In essence large trash piles created by generations of riverside clam bakes, these middens represent a sort of prehistoric architecture that enlightens us as to the lifestyles and diet of peoples who left us no written records.

Life among eastern North America's native groups underwent another series of paradigm-shifting changes beginning about AD 1000 so complete and transformative that we think of them as marking the beginning of an entire new era of regional human history. The Tensaw would come to occupy an especially prominent chapter in that story during what is known as the Mississippian period, playing host to one of the largest communities along the Gulf Coast, indeed the entire Southeast, along a tributary called Bottle Creek. Its story may just be the greatest of the Tensaw's many legends.

The Mississippian period, so named in reference to the fact that many of its hallmark practices, traditions, and technologies originated in the Mississippi valley and from there spread outward across much of the continent, lasted just a brief handful of centuries in comparison to the epochs that preceded it. In truth life during the time in many ways resembled those antecedent centuries. Yet in fundamental ways it can be characterized as a radical break in native life since it demarcated a gradual change in capacity and scale on many levels. Crops were more intensively cultivated in larger plots, community-wide building projects were entered into on a scope previously unknown, and elaborate rituals as a part of widespread shared religious beliefs became a core organizing force among the native population region-wide. The production of corn, especially, became a bedrock agricultural practice that ensured a stable food supply; high in calories and easily stored, it fueled the rise of Mississippian society. What all this meant in practical terms was that ever-larger groups of people could stay in one place for a longer period of time—yielding towns of several hundred or even several thousand people—a development made possible in part by an emergent stratified society wherein laborers tasked with production of essentials equipped the many. The shared bonds of ecclesiastical practice and worldview linked these

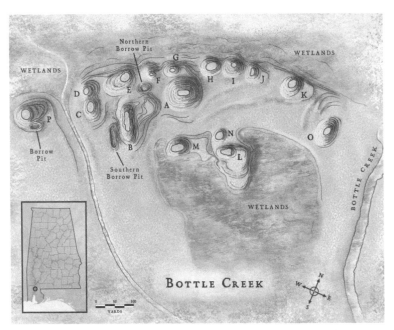

Map of the Bottle Creek Mound Complex. Courtesy of the Alabama Archives and History Foundation, Montgomery.

Panorama of Mound A, Bottle Creek complex. Courtesy of Mike Bunn.

communities together on philosophical levels barely contemplated in many places before.

Their trademark engineering accomplishments are a wonder to behold. Earthen mounds, some enormous and towering over their surrounding landscape and others more modest in size but equally rich in cultural import, serve as enduring reminders of the former presence of the Mississippian societies. While mound complexes are found throughout the greater Gulf region, there are two especially prominent in Alabama, and they stand as the only two prehistoric National Historic Landmarks in the state. One, known as Moundville, is located along the banks of the Black Warrior River just south of Tuscaloosa. Encompassing nearly two hundred acres and some twenty-nine mounds, it was once home to a community

of as many as 10,000 people living both at the mound center itself and in the adjacent river valley. The community is believed to have reached its peak size and influence around 1300. The Moundville site is owned by the University of Alabama and operated as a historic site and museum. As such, it is pristinely preserved, maintained, and interpreted and is unquestionably Alabama's best-known and most thoroughly studied Mississippian mound complex.

On the polar opposite end of the development spectrum lies the second largest mound complex in the state, and the largest anywhere on the north-central Gulf Coast—the fabled Bottle Creek Mound Complex along the quiet banks of the Tensaw. The site is located on Mound Island, a piece of land in the remotest reaches of the Delta several hundred acres in size bounded by the Tensaw on the north, Bottle Creek on its east and south, and sluggish Dominic Creek—part stream and part dreary, expansive swamp—on the west. The site, owned and monitored by state authorities, is completely undeveloped and accessible only by boat, an abandoned historic site in the raw where the natural environment in which it was birthed and nurtured is on glorious display. It is a place of wonder and inspiration for all those intrigued with the area's human history, in part because of what we know about it and in part because so much of its story remains to be told.

The quantifiable facts concerning the site are impressive. The Bottle Creek complex contains some nineteen confirmed earthen mounds built between about 1200 and 1600 and at its height would have been the centerpiece of a community of well over 1,000 people living in and around the mound center and all along the shores of nearby streams. The mounds are of course the lone extant feature of this dynamic prehistoric urban landscape. Concentrated in an area just under fifty acres in size, most are what archaeologists refer to as platform mounds, on top of which would have once stood wooden structures such as homes and temples. Several are relatively small, just a few feet high and appearing as low-rising humps on the thickly vegetated plain. A few are larger and more easily discernible, however. The largest, known as Mound A, is one of the most famous and historically rich landmarks in the entire Gulf Coast region. The mound is a physically impressive, monumental structure, which stands in silent testimony to the incredible amount of labor the community's leaders could marshal and the sophistication of their society. Adjacent to it, in a wide, flat expanse bordered by four other mounds, would have been what we today

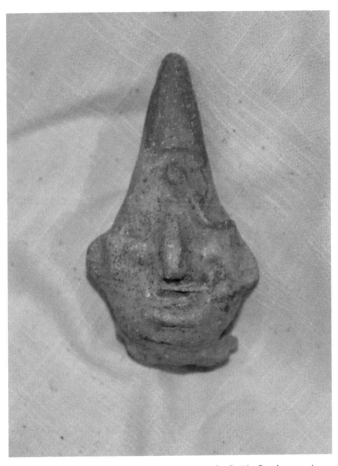

Human head effigy discovered in excavations at the Bottle Creek mound complex. Courtesy of the University of Alabama Center for Archaeological Studies, photography by the History Museum of Mobile.

Duck tail-shaped pottery fragment discovered in excavations at the Bottle Creek mound complex. Courtesy of the University of Alabama Center for Archaeological Studies, photography by the History Museum of Mobile.

refer to as a plaza. There are at least three large borrow pits on the island, where a portion of the soil used in the construction of the mounds was unearthed. Today they manifest themselves as small barren depressions in the heavy undergrowth, which periodically transform into shallow ponds in periods of high water.

Archaeologists have not studied the site to the degree they would like. In fact by some measures Bottle Creek ranks among the lesser-investigated major mound centers in the Southeast. This is not owing to any lack of interest, but rather, to the difficulties inherent in mustering the financial and logistical resources requisite for conducting major archaeological operations in a remote, semitropical floodplain situated in one of the rainiest locations in North America that is accessed solely by water. What has been learned from the pioneering efforts of scientists and academicians of various backgrounds, though, forms the core of the body of knowledge we have about the site. The mound site was mapped as early as the 1850s, and narrowly focused excavations took place on the island on at least two occasions in the early 1900s. By far the most substantial scientific exploration of the site occurred in the 1990s. Under the auspices of the University of South Alabama's Center for Archaeological Studies the site was professionally mapped during that time, while the University of Alabama's Gulf Coast Survey conducted the most thorough excavations ever attempted at the site under the direction of Dr. Ian Brown.

From these teams and those who have helped analyze what they have found, we have gained vital clues about everyday life at the mound center, which substantially helps us develop an informed mental picture of the place at its peak. Details of the construction of the mounds, the size and design of the homes built by the site's residents, the form and composition of the pottery they used in the preparation and storage of food, as well as the wide variety of shell, bone, and stone tools they fashioned have all been brought to light. In answer to some of the most fundamental questions those curious about life in centuries past ask, we have also learned that they dined on copious amounts of corn, fresh and brackish water clams, and fish as key parts of a fairly diverse diet.

But cold facts about day-to-day life along the Tensaw in centuries past do not tell us all we want to know about who these people really were or how they conceived themselves and their relationship to the riverine region that they called home.

In truth, most visitors to Bottle Creek find what is not yet known about the site as alluring as any of what can be measured, counted, or even confirmed. Every aspect of a visit to the site sparks the curious mind. Its location itself is unusual and gives rise to profound questions about how the site came to be a major population center. A trip to the island, along the serpentine course of the Tensaw and down the wide and deep creek that gives it its name, is provocative. There is no prominent bluff or open clearing that strikes one as an obvious place where human civilization would thrive, and no majestic architectural wonder looming in the visible distance to announce your arrival at a ruin. Traipsing through the murky, damp and tangled forest on the way to the mound center on one of the guided tours offered by Historic Blakeley State Park or private groups, one crosses streambeds –mudholes in dry weather and swift-flowing channels in wet—and advances through a veritable sea of palmetto. Nothing about it is typical of what we know of major Mississippian mound centers elsewhere, which are usually located on higher and drier lands. Many of the smaller mounds at Bottle Creek are hidden in the jungle-like, subtropical growth along the way to Mound A. Visitors to the island are reminded at every step along their journey, as well, that the Delta's regular inundations must have dictated a seasonal occupancy by most of its residents. Why, then, is it here? Where did its people come from, and why did they make the effort it surely took to live and build in this environment?

Upon at last reaching the heart of mound complex after the nearly half-mile trek from Bottle Creek, visitors finally encounter a grand memorial of the type they had expected in the form of Mound A—the largest earthwork on the island. With each step closer the enormous scale of Mound A comes into better view, a truly monumental structure supremely out of place in its surroundings. Its sight gives pause, and spurs more questions. What did this

Guided tour of the mound complex at Bottle Creek. Courtesy of Mike Bunn.

Tour group climbing Mound A. Tribal descendant communities have requested visitors not ascend the mound since this photograph was taken. It is shown here to help readers get a sense of scale. Courtesy of Mike Bunn.

place look like in its heyday? How and why was it constructed? Mound A rises some forty-five feet above the Delta marsh and would have stood as the awe-inspiring focal point of a settlement that commanded power and influence over a large region. In the 1300s or 1400s, when much of the surrounding trees and vegetation would have been cleared, it surely would have been a remarkable man-made landmark unlike anything that could be found for hundreds of miles in any direction. The mound was not built at one time but rather in numerous short stages taking place over the course of generations. One basketful of dirt, sand, and clay at a time, it took shape through the labor of perhaps thousands of hands. Hereditary chieftains led the Bottle Creek community during each era in which the larger complex took shape. They possessed the power to not only keep these earthworks maintained but to cause them to be enlarged and new ones brought into existence. Symbolically and literally, these chieftains sat above the people they ruled. Just as Mound A served as a political epicenter of sorts, so did the adjacent plaza it helped demarcate serve as a spiritual one, for important religious ceremonies and traditions took place on these grounds of which we have only the most rudimentary of understandings.

We may never know all that we would like about the Bottle Creek mound complex, and in the attempt to understand it in its fullness one is forced into the intellectual space where verified fact meets informed speculation. Lest we think we can know all about this place, it is worth remembering we have no idea even of the name its residents gave it. The origins of the mound center to this day are a topic of speculation. Most archaeologists believe it may have begun as an expansion of the chiefdom headquartered at Moundville, but there are clear indications of contact with the peoples of the lower Mississippi valley at an early date in the artifacts that have been recovered. The exact nature and purpose of the mound complex have yet to be demonstrated conclusively. Bottle Creek appears to have been a sort of outpost serving as a gateway into the region's interior river system, a physical reminder of power and influence and perhaps an important center of trade and exchange. But questions about its cosmological meaning to the people who developed and occupied it may be harder to document. Native American legends about the creation of the earth abound with stories of mythical creatures that, in a distant past where only animals of the air and water existed, worked together to form a literal middle ground on which humans would one day reside. Could mounds such as those at Bottle Creek have carried symbolic significance as tributes to the earth-forming powers of legendary beings such as crawfish? Might the spot chosen for the construction of this complex have had meaning beyond the utilitarian, perhaps chosen despite its obstacles in homage to or directly because of an earlier people or event? We may never know, but that is in some ways part of the enduring mystique of the place.

Bottle Creek's decline is wrapped in almost as many questions as those surrounding its rise. The arrival of European explorers in the region beginning in the mid-sixteenth century brought with it the spread of a host of diseases to which native groups had no immunity and led to horrific levels of depopulation. As much as 90 percent of the native population in the region perished during the ensuing waves of uncontrolled epidemics; the mind's eye conjures up struggling, disease-ridden villages along the Tensaw laid waste as pestilence ravaged their ability to secure and process food or protect themselves from desperate rivals. Perhaps all this and a panoply of other heartrending scenes played out along the Tensaw in the 1500s, but archaeologists have helped us understand other, less specific, factors must also be considered. Mound centers across the South were already in decline by the time European intruders first sailed into the Gulf's warm waters, their populations diminishing for a host of reasons we are still trying to uncover. Did chieftains have their power to command labor and resources undermined by a changing climate that transformed agricultural surpluses into devastating shortages? Had overuse of regional resources reached a point where their continued rates of extraction could no longer be sustained? It may be that all this and more led to the cessation of mound-building at the Bottle Creek complex and the dispersion of its population over what must have been an incredibly tumultuous century of decline and reorganization that ranks among the most profound occurrences in the history of the Gulf South.

Whatever the root cause or causes, by the time the colonial era opened in the Delta at the dawn of the eighteenth century, the settlement at Bottle Creek had long ceased to exist as a functioning community. It still carried cultural importance among the descendants of the Mississippian peoples who then called the region home, though. In 1702, Jean Baptiste Lemoyne de Bienville, brother of the founder of Mobile and governor of the colony of Louisiana Pierre Lemoyne d'Iberville, paid a visit to the site after hearing of it from Native Americans in the new town the French were laying out a few miles to the southwest. He wanted to see, as he recorded in a letter he later wrote about the trip, "the place where their gods are." Bribing a Mobilian Indian with a musket to guide him, he discovered what he took to be a sort of shrine on one of the mounds, which even then had been obscured by a century of reclamation of natural growth. He absconded with five effigies—of a man, a woman, a child, a bear, and an owl—which he sent back to France as souvenirs of his explorations. The Mobilians professed astonishment that he had not been struck dead as a result of such trespassing and wanton plunder. The items Bienville referenced have long been lost to history, and their origin and purpose remain unclear. Regardless, their discovery and the Mobilians' reaction to the event demonstrates clearly that the mound site, even if long abandoned, continued to be held in high regard generations after its days as a functioning community. Today the Choctaws, the Creeks, and other Indigenous groups regard it and other similar mound sites as physical connections to distant shared ancestors. For that reason alone among many, Bottle Creek will remain a sacred place and continue to occupy an especially important spot in the Tensaw's rich cultural heritage.[1]

3

Age of Empire

I N COMPARISON TO THE ICONIC MONUMENTAL ARCHITEC-
ture left behind by the Mississippian residents of the Tensaw, virtually nothing stands from the settlements later Europeans created
along the slow-rolling river. French, British, and Spanish colonial
eras would come and go in Tensaw country over the course of a little over a century between about 1700 and 1800, each characterized by different approaches to enlarging colonial empires through
the embellishment of local hegemony. Each, in turn, met with a
multitude of reverses in the attempt, and featured long periods of
little or no growth punctuated by moments of triumph before a
sudden, calamitous collapse that ushered in a new epoch. The colonial period along the Tensaw is interesting for many reasons, not
the least of which is its remarkable confluence of competing international agendas and an unprecedented mixing of Europeans, Africans, and Indigenous peoples on the river's humid banks. The era is
marked by stories of ability and inefficiency, flourishment and suffering, endurance and frailty.

When Bienville ventured to Mound Island to see for himself the curious shrine of which he had heard so much talk, he

was already heavily involved in laying the foundations for what would become the first serious colonial effort in the Delta region. The French expedition under d'Iberville had landed on the Gulf Coast in 1699 seeking a place from which they could wrest a new colony from the southeastern forests that would at long last make good René-Robert Cavelier, Sieur de La Salle's 1682 claim of the entirety of the Mississippi valley for France. The brazen assertion disregarded centuries of Native occupation dating back thousands of years. Temporarily settling on what is now the Mississippi Gulf Coast, the French began extensive exploration of the coastal region at once, and at length determined the best place for a permanent town might just be considerably farther inland. On what we now know as 27-Mile Bluff along the Mobile River, a few miles west of the gently flowing waters of the Tensaw, they began construction in 1702 of the original city of Mobile and its centerpiece, Fort Louis de la Louisiane. It would become the first capital of the boldly expansive colony of Louisiana, which, at least on paper, stretched from the Gulf up into what is now America's Midwest.

The French had not been the first to dream of establishing empire on the Gulf Coast. Spurred by advances in shipbuilding and navigation technology, lured by the promise of the expansion of lucrative trade networks and the discovery of precious metals, and seeking to embellish their sponsoring nations' international standing and spread their version of Christianity to every corner of the globe, European explorers had sailed into Mobile Bay as early as 1519. The most celebrated of those who traveled through the greater Gulf Coast region, without doubt, is Hernando de Soto. During an extended journey in pursuit of riches and glory, he and the hundreds of men he commanded trekked across the Deep South and into the pages of history between 1539 and 1542. Other expeditions would follow, smaller in scale yet equally ambitious, although none ended up establishing anything permanent in this New World prior to the small party of interlopers who labored under the fleur-de-lis flag.

Those previous forays had nonetheless played an important part in significantly altering the cultural landscape into which the French would attempt to establish themselves. For starters, they had unwittingly helped initiate cycles of disease and disruption among Mississippian populations that would devastate these communities and end in their transition into smaller distinct tribal entities with defined, permanent territorial borders. The Tensaw's colonial era opened while this transformation was still very much in process. Instead of the Choctaw and Creek as they would be known a generation later, for example, the French met with many smaller groups of semi-independent people they called "petites [little] nations." Their lineage, traditions, and extent of authority were connected to all that had existed previously in the area, yet distinct enough to be remembered as evidence of a regional shift in communal organization that can be understood as a transitory middle ground from one type of civilization to another.

These native peoples would play a critical role in the success of the Gallic colonial enterprise among the Delta's thickly forested recesses and along the sandy shores of the Gulf. They informed the French about the region's geography and peoples, provided military aid in occasional emergency, served as valued trading partners, and, most critically of all, provided much of the food that sustained the French and allowed them to persist in the region despite lack-luster ability or commitment in agricultural endeavors. In fact it was the desire to be in proximity to these valuable allies, not any inherent strategic importance of the site itself, that influenced the French to build the original town of Mobile near the home of the Mobilian Indians for whom they named the place. They also made friends with the Tomes, who lived along the southernmost reaches of the Tombigbee at the time, and encouraged the immigration to the region of another petite nation from Spanish Florida known as the Apalachee. Driven to desperation by raids on their villages by the British and their Creek allies, they were welcomed by the French in the attempt to found a new home in the Mobile Bay area. In the first decade of the eighteenth century they organized at least two villages along the banks of the Mobile River and in the 1730s established a town on a bluff overlooking the Tensaw on the site of what would some 250 years later become Historic Blakeley State Park. Practicing Catholics as a result of conversion to Christianity by Spanish missionaries a generation earlier, these peoples would come to play an important part in the cultural and economic life of the young colony the French were striving to create.

The Tensaw owes its very name to yet another native group welcomed into the area in the first years of the establishment of the new French colony. The Taensa (sometimes spelled Tensas, Tensa, and rarely, Tensaw) migrated to the Delta area from what is now Louisiana around 1715. They are documented in the ear-liest French explorations of the lower Mississippi valley as having lived in seven villages and for a time had a Catholic mission within their territory. When epidemics of disease and raids by other, more powerful tribes ravaged the Taensa in much the same manner as the Apalachee in the first decade of the eighteenth century, they determined to relocate eastward in part to enjoy the protection of their newfound French allies. Taensa guides had rendered valuable support to the French by helping them understand the political geography of the land they were attempting to colonize. They had even helped them get their hands on a troublesome interloper named Pryce Hughes who, before his murder at the hands of the warriors of another allied petite nation, had envisioned a Welsh colony in the area the French were attempting to bring under their influence. In return for their assistance and friendship, the French encouraged their immigration to the Mobile area. By the early 1720s, they had settled on the banks of the river that would soon bear their name. Their residency along the storied river would be relatively brief, though. Shortly after the French were forced to abandon the colony in the wake of their defeat at the hands of Great Britain in the Seven Years' War in 1763, the Taensa returned to their Louisiana home.

The courting of the Taensa is just one manifestation of the commitment of the French to their ultimately failed effort to build a permanent Gulf Coast colony. Through government auspices and via private companies operating on its behalf, they labored with purpose to shape the region in their image for over six decades. Despite a continual, debilitating, lack of resources, a small number of able individuals managed to meet with no small measure of success in solidifying relationships with more populous Native groups and defending their borders from the intrusions of the more powerful British and the opportunistic Spanish. That commitment is in part

Maps of the Tensaw region during the French (*top*), British (*middle*), and Spanish (*bottom*) periods. Courtesy of the David Rumsey Map Collection.

why the French legacy endures in numerous place names from Mobile to New Orleans, and why we remember their pioneering efforts as a vital part of the Gulf Coast region's colorful past. But for every advance made by the French, they seemed to suffer counterbalancing setbacks in their efforts to make their colony a thriving, independent enterprise. The far-flung and cash-strapped outpost drew relatively few willing immigrants, and the difficult living conditions in its founding era remained a constant for most of its population right up until its transfer to the British as a prize of a war waged far from its shores. Among the small portion of the population that managed to find any degree of economic success in this area of the colony of Louisiana were the planters who operated the scattered plantations powered by the labor of the enslaved Africans the French had introduced to the region. Clustered on the Mobile River at first, they would introduce a type of economic activity to the larger region that would soon find its way across the Delta to the banks of the Tensaw.

Believing they could do better than their predecessors in the furtherance of empire in southeastern North America's humid coastal plain, Great Britain moved quickly to establish the colonies of West and East Florida in the southernmost swath of territory it acquired through victory in the Seven Years' War. The province of West Florida stretched from the Mississippi in the west to the Apalachicola in the east and was bordered by the Gulf of Mexico in the south and the 31st parallel (later moved to 32′ 28″) in the north. The Delta lay virtually dead center in the geography of this new political entity that would grace world maps during one of the most consequential periods of development in all of the region's long history. During this brief interlude, the Tensaw would emerge as a destination for Europeans and Africans as never before.

Accounts from those employed in creating the colony and others who visited it during the process highlight both the region's challenges and charm. Many officials and troops, perceiving themselves assigned to duty on a forgotten, ragged edge of civilization, decried the place as an impoverished and pestilence-ridden backwater. Hyperbole aside, there was some truth behind the allegation that the environs of Mobile were, as one British official put it, little more than "a grave yard for Britons." Disease ran rampant among the newly arrived troops. Frighteningly high morbidity manifested itself among the poorly nourished, closely quartered men in the first years of British administration in the Delta region as they succumbed to an assortment of communicable diseases in the unfamiliar and unforgiving climate. Internationally noted naturalist Bernard Romans, whose experiences in the colony are preserved in the landmark publication titled *A Concise Natural History of East and West Florida*, expressed astonishment at the searing heat of the region in summer. Almost as a warning to potential settlers, he pointed an accusing finger toward it as the cause of "sudden rarefactions of the humours" among the suffering residents. On the other hand stand the writings of early America's most famous observer of the natural environment, William Bartram. He journeyed through the Delta and along the placid Tensaw in 1775 as part of an extended trek across the Southeast, which would later result in the treasured piece of American literature titled *Travels*. Bartram marveled at the "Canes and Cypress trees of an astonishing magnitude" he found along the Delta's labyrinthine waterways and stood enthralled by "the stately columns of the Magnolia grandiflora" he found thriving in the black soil. He expressed rapture at finding a new species of evening primrose on his Tensaw adventure, proclaiming it "perhaps the most pompous and brilliant herbaceous plant yet known to exist." Totally mesmerized by the natural

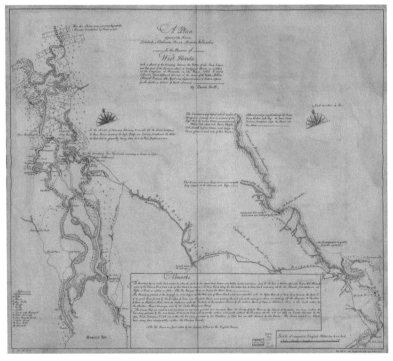

"A Plan of part of the Rivers Tombecbe, Alabama, Tensa, Perdido, and Scambia," by David Taitt, 1771. Courtesy of the Library of Congress.

Robert Farmar owned a well-known plantation on the banks of the Tensaw. Courtesy of the Alabama Department of Archives and History, Montgomery.

William Bartram, early America's most famed naturalists, visited the Tensaw in the 1770s. Courtesy of the Library of Congress.

bounty surrounding him, he excitedly summarized his visit to the Delta's streams and bottomland forests by exclaiming, "What a sylvan scene is here!"[1]

In this lush but demanding landscape settlers, some the descendants of some of the first French arrivals in the area and others from near and far, arrived to try their hand at wresting a living from the fertile banks that channeled the Tensaw toward the sea. Immigration never reached the levels the British had hoped and dreamed during their administration of West Florida, but a steady trickle of newcomers, drawn by the promise of cheap, productive land, washed up on the region's shores from other North American colonies, British holdings in the Caribbean, and even a small number directly from Europe. A majority toiled to produce enough food for themselves and their families and hoped to have an excess that could be brought to market. Many, though, arrived with African slaves in tow or purchased them once here from traders, initiating the first widespread manifestation of the plantation labor system that would come to play such a fundamental role in the larger region's economy for the next century. Some of these plantations were modest affairs of a few dozen riverside acres where a lone family resided; others were much larger tracts on which bondsmen worked crops and tended livestock under the oversight of a hired supervisor while the owner of the property maintained a primary residence in Mobile. The scale and scope of most of these enterprises paled in comparison to anything the word "plantation" might connote as it applies to the antebellum South, however. Still, the forced labor they required was just as brutal.

Under the broiling summer sun and wrapped in a virtual blanket of humidity, enslaved laborers on Tensaw River plantations felled trees, prepared fields, and constructed homes, outbuildings, and barns in some of the first efforts of their type along the waterway's course. By hard labor they cultivated an abundance of corn and sweet potatoes, a considerable amount of chickpeas and pumpkins, and other crops including rice, peas, sugarcane, and a variety of other fruits and vegetables including apples, plums, lemons, oranges, pears, peaches, grapes, figs, melons, onions, and radishes. A few operators of these plantations pursued economic success through having laborers undertake production of tobacco and indigo, but with only mediocre results due to the difficulty involved in the multistep processes of production and the gaining of access to competitive international markets. The steadiest sources of profits for many farmers and plantation owners alike eventually proved to come through herding, lumbering, and naval stores production. Milk, butter, and meat were always in demand in colonial communities. Wood from the area's plentiful stands of timber supplied the material for building homes, furniture, and the crates and barrels in which items were transported overseas, while pitch, tar, and pine were marketable commodities in the age of sailing ships.

By the 1770s the Tensaw had become a nascent colonial agricultural district, showcasing scattered farm clearings buzzing with activity along portions of its winding route all the way from the upper Delta to the bay. Most of those overlooking the river's northernmost and southernmost reaches lay some distance from their neighboring properties. Along the Tensaw's middle reaches, though, where the rolling, verdant forestland met a series of modest bluffs rising above the floodplain, lay a cluster of home-steads locally known as the "Tensaw Settlement." Standing in the middle of this pocket community was one of the best-documented plantations along the river in the colonial era, known as Farm Hall. It belonged to British military officer Robert Farmar, who had pur-chased the property from French settlers a few years after his ar-rival in West Florida and soon set about creating one of the most well-appointed establishments of its type anywhere in the colony. Farm Hall eventually grew to encompass hundreds of acres, a por-tion of which were under constant cultivation by over four dozen enslaved individuals. At its center stood Farmar's massive home, a regional landmark of sorts that would become noted by multi-ple visitors to the region for the lavish hospitality practiced by its owners, including no less a figure than William Bartram. Its fur-nishings demonstrated Farmar's unusual wealth. On display in the home were a large library, a collection of expensive furniture, and walls decorated with a variety of military mementos Farmar had collected over the course of his career.

The American Revolution would bring a sudden end to Brit-ish efforts to develop their Gulf Coast colony, but not owing to any American opposition to Crown government. West Florida is usu-ally labeled as a loyal colony in histories of the war owing to the fact it did not rebel against its home government, and is dismissed as inconsequential because little campaigning took place between the patriot and British armies in the area. But the war found the area nonetheless. An international conflict pitting Great Britain against Spain, which had inherited trans-Mississippi Louisiana from the French when they left the region, would be waged for control of the fledgling colony of West Florida. The Tensaw would figure only tangentially in the fighting, which raged from the shores of the Mississippi to Pensacola Bay between 1779 and 1781, but the events that occurred in its vicinity stand as a unique if all but forgotten connection to our nation's tumultuous founding era.

A Spanish army under the command of Louisiana governor Bernardo de Galvez arrived outside of the walls of Fort Charlotte in Mobile in March 1780 with the intent to capture the place. A British relief column rushed to the Tensaw from Pensacola in hopes of relieving the siege arrived too late to avert the city's fall, however. On the eastern shore of Mobile Bay in January 1781, Spanish and British forces squared off at a little crossroads farming community known as The Village, again resulting in victory for the Spaniards. When the capital of Pensacola fell later that year to Galvez's army, all West Florida became a part of the Spanish Empire.

Its sweeping victory over the British notwithstanding, Spain was actually on the decline as a world power when it acquired West Florida via stunning military conquest. It would struggle mightily to obtain the troops, equipment, and financial resources necessary to improve and develop its new colony in the years ahead. Even though it made remarkable progress in constructing fortifications to protect its borders, forging alliances with Native societies, encouraging immigration through liberal land concessions, and conciliating existing residents of French and British extraction with mild government, Spanish authority would later crumble before the upstart Americans.

The first step in Spain's collapse involved the colony's contested northern boundary. The Spanish had attempted to hold the borders the British had observed, but the United States insisted the 31st parallel, as originally called for back in the first Treaty of Paris of 1763 ending the Seven Years' War and reaffirmed in the compact of the same name establishing American independence two decades later, as the demarcation of the new international borderline. The Spanish preferred 32' 28 minutes, the northern boundary of West Florida established by the British in 1764. Spain reluctantly acceded in a treaty signed in 1795, but did not withdraw southward until 1798. As fast as congressional procedure would allow, the United States established a province in the long-contested region—the Mississippi Territory. America's preeminent surveyor, Pennsylvania-born Andrew Ellicott, led the team that marked the new boundary, trudging across the pulsing waterways and tangled swamps of the Delta as they made their way from the Mississippi to the Chattahoochee and through the lands of the Creek Nation to document the new line. The boundary bisected the Tensaw itself, leaving a few miles of its northernmost reaches in the new American Territory but over two-thirds of its course still in Spanish hands. The line would become an ephemeral focal point in an international contest for control of the Gulf Coast between the United States and Spain.

The spark for American immigration into the region proved to be an ingenious mechanical invention by a man named Eli Whitney. His machine, easily replicated by numerous others in the Gulf Coast region, made it possible to process enormous amounts of cotton for the first time. The fiber was starting to come into high demand in the textile mills of Europe and New England, and the lands of the Mississippi Territory happened to be one of the places most conducive to its cultivation. On both sides of the border along the Tensaw, the crop promised to become the long-sought agricultural staple that had been pursued doggedly, but for the most part vainly, by settlers of three colonial regimes. Americans flocking to the region deeply resented foreign control of the gulf outlets of the rivers that flowed through their southwestern frontier, however. Their government yielded aid to their efforts to eliminate such an artificial obstacle to financial success, manufacturing claims to the region through diplomacy, looking the other way as extralegal methods were applied to wrest the region from the Spanish, and applying direct pressure of its own with the goal of expanding American control all the way to the Gulf. The end of the Spanish era along the Tensaw would come in just a decade and a half after the withdrawal south of the 31st parallel and usher in a dynamic new era of conflict and expansion.

4

Opening of the American Era

THE AMERICAN ERA ALONG THE TENSAW BEGAN WITH A TU-multuous interlude of extralegal pressure being applied to the European owners of its southern reaches. Rather than one single watershed moment, the "Americanization" of the Tensaw involved a dizzying series of political maneuvers, military clashes, and internal struggles, which altogether would form one of the most complex and decisive periods in its long history. At its end the Tensaw River would become a thoroughly American corridor featuring one of the young state of Alabama's largest urban centers perched along its banks.

In 1810 an ominous threat to Spain's control of the colony of West Florida began over 200 miles west of the Tensaw, in Baton Rouge. There, a group of Americans living in the region staged a coup that overthrew local colonial authority. Establishing what they called the independent "Republic of West Florida," they shortly after sent emissaries to the Mobile area charged with encouraging people there to join them in ousting the Spanish from the remainder of the colony. In November 1810, a small army of West Florida Republic patriot "conventioners" gathered along the Tensaw opposite Mobile.

They chose as their rallying point a rise called McCurtin's (or Fisher's) Bluff near the Tensaw Settlement, which they referred to as "Bunker's Hill" in a grandiloquent reference to the supposed revolutionary nature of their mission. There they raised the new republic's lone star flag on Sunday, November 25, 1810, and went about purportedly preparing for a hostile takeover of Mobile through the rallying of a pro–West Florida military force. But their actions were marked by considerably more bluster than substance. No citizen army rushed to their colors, and nobody but the Spanish authorities in Mobile seemed to know exactly what to do next about this sputtering, bloviating rebellion. On the night of December 10, 1810, the Spaniards advanced on the would-be revolutionary army, which had by then shrunk in size and moved its base to the banks of a small stream just north of Mobile known as Saw Mill Creek. On their stealthy approach, the Spanish troops found the erstwhile rebels in the middle of a drunken frolic. In a brief exchange of gunfire, which studded the black night with the bright orange blazes of sparking powder, the attackers killed at least four men and captured ten more, scattering the remainder in disorder. Two Spaniards fell dead in the melee. Spain had stymied the weak-willed attempt to take their Delta lands by force, at least for the moment.

But the would-be rebellion was just the first step in a saga of piecemeal American acquisition between 1810 and 1813. Justifying its actions in a somewhat specious claim that the region belonged to the United States by virtue of the terms of the Louisiana Purchase, through acts passed by Congress, America officially annexed the territory overtaken by rebels around Baton Rouge into the new state of Louisiana and laid claim to the remainder of West

Florida between the Pearl and Perdido Rivers. It went so far as to add that section of the colony to the Mississippi Territory even though Spain did not recognize these claims as legal and continued to maintain a garrison in Mobile. During the War of 1812 the United States at last came into undisputed possession of the area when on April 12, 1813, General James Wilkinson arrived at Mobile with a large combined army and navy force and demanded the surrender of Fort Carlota. Severely outnumbered, its commander, Captain Cayetano Perez, did so without firing a shot the next day. At last, the entire length of the Tensaw and the large Delta and Mobile Bay region lay in American hands.

Virtually as soon as ownership of this frontier region changed hands, it became the unlikely theater for the opening act of a cataclysmic drama that would chart a new course in regional history. The fertile bottomlands drained by the Tensaw lay on the far southwestern edges of the ancestral domain at the time claimed by the Creeks, and stood as a border region separating their hunting lands from the neighboring Choctaws. The Creeks had allowed its settlement by Americans specifically because the region lay relatively removed from the heart of their homeland. American settlers and their slaves poured into the area beyond expectations, though, swelling the population and transforming it into a patchwork of rural homesteads, farms, and plantations over the course of little more than a decade. Many of them arrived via an arduous trip down the new Federal Road, which had been designed to connect Washington, DC, and New Orleans. The route cut through the region and, via ferry, across the Delta on its way to Fort Stoddert. A branch of the route ran roughly parallel to the Tensaw as it connected Mims'

Ferry with points south, through a developing community a short distance from the river that would loom large in its territorial period saga. By 1813 "The Tensaw," as it had become known, stood as a region unto itself in the emerging Mississippi Territory, home to a growing population of both Americans and Creeks who were living very similar lifestyles out of the orbit of the primary tribal towns to the northeast. Despite the fact it featured no concentrated urban centers, the Tensaw region ranked as one of largest areas of clustered settlements in the entire Territory.

Long-simmering internal tensions among the Creeks over their rather one-sided interactions with the growing United States and its land-hungry citizens were coming to a boil in the first decade of the nineteenth century. In the fall of 1811 the charismatic Shawnee leader Tecumseh traveled from his home in the Great Lakes region to encourage the Southeastern tribes to join him in reclaiming their ancestral ways by resisting further American expansion and influence in their lands. Tecumseh proved to be the spark that transformed a disorganized political vision into a focused religious crusade among a faction of the Creek Nation that felt their future as a people imperiled by continued accommodation. In the coming months, Red Sticks, so named for the red war clubs that symbolized their willingness to consider any measure—including war if necessary—to reclaim their cultural autonomy began intimidating kinsmen who did not join their cause. The ensuing civil war among the Creeks threatened to engulf the entire early American Southwest in fiery conflict. Alarm spread throughout the Mississippi Territory among its American settlements. Nowhere was the perceived threat more immediate than in the Tensaw country.

Several makeshift forts were hastily erected around farms and mills in the lower Alabama/Tombigbee/Tensaw region in the summer of 1813 to which area settlers fled as the Creek's internecine conflict escalated. American fears that the quarrel might spill over into a more general war rose as the stockades filled. Just to the northeast of the junction where the Mobile and the Tensaw rivers split, near an old oxbow of the Alabama, stood one such outpost, constructed around the plantation home and outbuildings of Samuel Mims. Anticipation became reality when the first clash in what proved to be the feared wider war occurred at a place called Burnt Corn Creek in late July. The fact that it actually had been a rather small skirmish brought on by opportunistic American militia easily got forgotten in the panic that followed as American settlers braced themselves for what they believed would be a vicious frontier war. On August 30, 1813, hundreds of Red Stick warriors led by William Weatherford, a wealthy and influential Creek born to a European father and a Creek mother, moved stealthily on the makeshift fortification known as Fort Mims preparatory to an attack in reprisal against their kinsmen who had fought alongside the Americans at Burnt Corn. The occupants of Fort Mims were caught completely off guard and nearly overwhelmed in a vicious riot of carnage before organizing a defense. They managed to halt the initial Red Stick onslaught with volleys of desperate gunfire after a frenzied few minutes of vicious close-quarters fighting, but the attackers launched a second assault later in the day that spelled doom for the fort. In the massacre that followed, Fort Mims was burned and the great majority of those in it were killed. About one hundred were taken captive with no more than thirty managing to make a frantic escape. The Red Sticks had won a stunning and complete victory. Immediately American armies were raised in the Mississippi Territory's neighboring states to put down what US officials characterized as a rebellion.

The Creek War continued to ripple down the Tensaw in the coming months. Its largest battles would be waged in what are now central and northeastern Alabama, with the decisive clash at Horseshoe Bend in March 1814 marking an abrupt end to active campaigning between the contending forces. On April 26, 1814, Tensaw River settler Gerald Byrne, who had abandoned his plantation after the fall of Fort Mims to seek refuge for his family, made a cautious return to his land to begin spring planting. Accompanied by only a few enslaved persons, he supposed the bitter conflict that had swept over the region had reached an end. A few days into the work some acquaintances joined him for a visit. At daybreak the morning after their arrival a group of Red Sticks descended on them, striking down Byrne and one of his friends before they could make any defense, and chasing down and killing and scalping another unfortunate man who had managed to escape the initial onslaught. One of Byrne's slaves also fell in the melee, but the Red Sticks took several others as their prisoners and absconded with a number of horses to boot. That the Creek War would soon be officially over and the incident along the middle reaches of the Tensaw would be the last of its type in the area were of little solace to the families of those slain. But they marked the final, tragic chapter in a region-wide bloodletting that ended one period in the river's human history and opened another.[1]

A few months prior to the affair at Byrne's plantation, the Mississippi territorial legislature incorporated a new town being planned just to its south. It would be called Blakeley in honor of its organizer, a native of Connecticut named Josiah Blakeley. Blakeley had washed up in Mobile in 1806, during the waning years of Spanish hegemony along the Gulf Coast, after a sojourn in Cuba where he served briefly as American consul. In his new home he quickly rose to prominence, serving in a variety of governmental posts and civic organizations, including spearheading the effort to

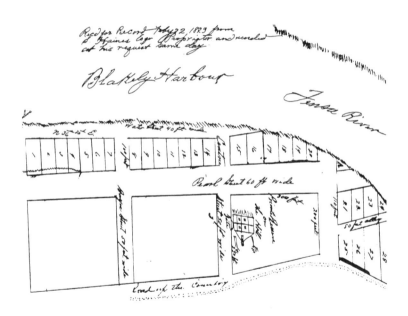

Plan of the Town of Blakeley, 1823. Courtesy of the Alabama Department of Archives and History, Montgomery.

incorporate Mobile as a city once it came into American possession. Blakeley busied himself in the cultivation of a plantation on the island he purchased shortly after arrival that today bears his name (Blakeley Island) opposite of Mobile. He called it "Festino," and it soon became the centerpiece of a thriving estate that included thousands of acres of Delta marsh on which lucrative crops and livestock were raised. But Blakeley's thoughts were focused on the future commercial possibilities of the greater Mobile Bay region, and for that his gaze was firmly fixed eastward, to the bluffs of the commodious Tensaw.

Josiah Blakeley was a dreamer and a schemer who recognized a good opportunity when he saw one. He could see that the pressure being applied by the burgeoning American nation to Spain's tenuous hold on the region would surely lead to a change of ownership. He may have not been the first to recognize the potential economic bonanza inherent in American control of both the entirety of the vast river systems draining some of the best cotton lands in the nation and their Gulf outlet at the head of Mobile Bay, but he determined to be among the first to capitalize on it. Blakeley figured there would surely be room for more than one port city in the capacious Delta watershed that offered easy connection to world markets. Plus, as a businessman he no doubt realized the shortcomings of Mobile's languishing harbor facilities and the hardships involved in navigation by ocean-going vessels attempting to do business in them. Troublesome shallows defined by muddy sandbars blocked easy direct access to Mobile's port prior to the era of extensive dredging, but the deep and wide Tensaw promised easier sailing once past the Dog River bar in the upper bay. Blakeley

DIED
in this place Dec 17 1844
JAMES W PETERS Esq
[illegible]
aged 51 Years
[illegible] with his partner
BASIL STEBBINS
emigrated from New York
to this Country in 1816
There was with a few other
[illegible] enterprising young
gentlemen from the North
concerned in the
delegate and founded the
town of Blakeley in 1817

Obelisk marking the graves of some of the founders of the town of Blakeley. Courtesy of History Blakeley State Park.

struck on an audacious plan to build a cross-Delta city to challenge Mobile for trade, population, and influence.

Blakeley eyed a long, low bluff on the Tensaw for his planned city, just north of where the Apalachee branches off toward Mobile Bay. He acquired the land from Dr. Joseph Chastang, a prominent local landowner who had held the property as part of his huge "White House" plantation from its earliest years as part of Spanish West Florida. As originally laid out, the town of Blakeley consisted of a grid of streets featuring two public squares situated along a bluff on the eastern bank of the Tensaw. The primary streets ran north–south and parallel to the river, while a series of shorter

Remains of the Baldwin County Courthouse, ca. 1900. Anna H. Rickarby Collection, the Doy Leale McCall Rare Book and Manuscript Library, University of South Alabama.

east–west crossing avenues and alleys extended between the river's edge and the broken ravine-filled terrain farther inland. According to lore, the main streets and avenues were named for political leaders of note in the era—Adams, Franklin, Greene, Wayne, Clinton, Baldwin, Hancock, Washington, and so on—while the lesser streets seem to have received their designations in honor of flora—Pine, Fig, Live Oak, Laurel. The town drew on numerous hillside springs for its water, which may have been piped into the town center. The town was incorporated by the Mississippi territorial legislature on January 6, 1814, with the first lots sold later that year. Tragically, Josiah Blakeley did not live to see his dreams for

These "ghost structures" help visitors to Historic Blakeley State Park better understand the built environment of the town that once stood on its grounds. Courtesy of Historic Blakeley State Park.

his namesake town come to pass, as he died in February 1815 after a short but severe illness. Yet his name would live on in the city he willed into being. It was an urban scene unlike anything ever witnessed along the venerable river, before or since.

By 1818 the booming town of Blakeley was already one of the largest cities in the Alabama Territory and seemingly on the path to continued ascendancy. Most estimates place Blakeley's population as only slightly less than Mobile at the time, perhaps approaching 1,000 residents. Over two dozen mercantile establishments where all manner of merchandise could be bought flanked its dirt streets as they cut their way under ancient live oaks. Two hotels offered accommodations to travelers, soon to include no less a visitor than Andrew Jackson while en route to become governor of the Florida Territory. Gabriel F. Mott's *Blakeley Sun and Alabama Advertiser* offered biweekly editions of one of Alabama's first newspapers. In the pages of the nearby *St. Stephens Halcyon* on February 22, 1819, an editorial described in rapturous tones the marvel of urban development at the burgeoning riverside metropolis:

> What a wonderful country is ours! How like enchantment towns and villages rise up! Blakeley eighteen months ago was a wilderness of impenetrable woods . . .—but now by the hardy and undaunted American; nothing is now seen or heard but the din of business and the stroke of the axe resounding through the distant woods— buildings raising their heads in almost every quarter of the town, and the constant arrival and

departure of vessels . . . We find no hesitation
in saying that Blakeley will before many years, be
the chief seaport town in the Alabama Territory.[2]

The allusion to the town's future being intertwined with the
Tensaw could not have been more accurate. Both its reason for

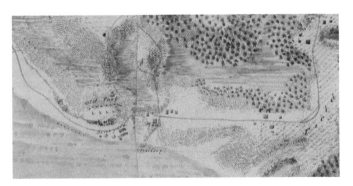

Section of *Blakeley: Its Environs, Approaches, and Defences*, drawn by Nicola
Marschall during the Civil War, showing what remained of the town of
Blakeley. Courtesy of the National Archives.

Blakeley Sun and Alabama Advertiser masthead. Courtesy of Historic Blakeley
State Park.

existence and its future prospects lay bound up with the ebb and flow of the mighty river's currents. Between 1817 and 1818 alone some sixty vessels called on the port, bringing in their holds goods from New Orleans, New England, and the West Indies. They left laden with the produce of the country: cotton, lumber, hogshead staves, hides, whiskey, beeswax, and tallow. Accentuating the pace of riverine trade were two major roads bringing goods and travelers, by wagon and coach, respectively, which terminated on Blakeley's riverside bluff. The town quickly became a harbor of some significance for the young state of Alabama, which entered the union in 1819, and won designation as an official port of entry. But the city became a hub of maritime activity in other ways, as well. One of the first steamboats to successfully navigate Alabama's rivers, the sternwheel *Tensas*, slid off its ways and splashed into its namesake waterway in 1819, the product of the pragmatically named Steamboat Company of Alabama. That company also constructed the *Mississippi*, a substantial vessel of 400 tons burden, a short time later. By 1820 local boat operator John Fowler had secured rights to operate a cross-Delta ferry, the *Emeline*, between Blakeley and Mobile.

A number of noted individuals whose names echo through Baldwin County history were associated with the town, calling the place home or being otherwise integrally involved in its coming of age: Haines, Carson, Toulmin, Byrne, Kennedy, Stockton, and Sibley among them. Blakeley's crowning achievement may have come in December 1820, when it was designated as the county seat of Baldwin County, a title it would hold until after the Civil War. But Blakeley went almost as fast as it came, the victim of recurring

waves of dreaded yellow fever, economic setbacks, runaway infla-
tion, improvements to the harbor facilities in rival Mobile, and at
least one devastating fire by 1830. Although it showed flickers of
life during the periodic sessions of court that continued to be held
there even as its homes and businesses were abandoned or disas-
sembled and moved away, Blakeley essentially ceased to exist as a
functioning town by 1840.

As is so often the case with stories of the distant past regardless
of location, legend and myth filled in holes in the historical record

The Tensaw River from the Blakeley Dock with downtown Mobile in the distance. Courtesy of Mike Bunn.

about Blakeley's rise. The cumulative effect has been, thankfully for those interested in heritage education, less abject disinformation than enduring intrigue about a remarkable but thinly documented story. Today Blakeley is a ghost town, its site part of a historic park where its story lives on through interpretive efforts and programming connecting visitors with a bygone era. A cemetery standing on its southeastern margins and containing the graves of some of its earliest residents bears silent testimony to the ephemeral nature of the long-vanished city.

According to Historic Blakeley State Park founding director Mary Grice, something profoundly real, if intangible, remains on the empty streets of old Blakeley today: "It is an air of mystery, a stateliness about the many grand oaks, a river scent that sharpens the imagination until one sees the creaky wagons rolling down cobbled streets to the waiting steamboats at the wharf. . . . There is an arrested excitement in these tangled woods and paths that tells even the unknowing visitor unfamiliar with the few historical facts available that something happened here a long time ago—or last year—or yesterday."[3]

5

The Spectacle of Battle

THE DEEP RUMBLE OF ARTILLERY FIRE BECAME THE AUDI-
tory backdrop to the surreal scene along the lower reaches of
the Tensaw near the old town of Blakeley throughout the first week
of April, 1865. On the ninth day of that month it reached a sudden
ear-splitting crescendo in the late afternoon, only to be followed by
brief lull. Then a cacophony of popping musketry and the dull roar
of thousands of voices reverberated across the river's dark waters.
Within a little more than a mere half hour of chaotic and deadly
combat between the contending armies arrayed for one of the final
battles in a war then entering its fifth spring, all had fallen quiet save
for an occasional desultory blast in the distance. The Battle of Fort
Blakeley was over, and another epic chapter in the story of the Tensaw had summarily closed.

As late as just a few months previous, Blakeley would have
seemed an unlikely spot indeed for a military contest the size of
that which occurred there in the last days of the Civil War. The decades between the town's decline in the 1830s and the beginning of
the Civil War had been largely uneventful, at least in comparison to
that of its rise, and gave no hint the place would ever again become

familiar to anyone outside its immediate environs. In the roughly three decades since it had been a population center of any size the former port city had melted away into the riverside forests and no longer stood as a recognizable community. Save for the small courthouse standing a few hundred feet from the Tensaw's timeless flow, the still-discernible but narrowing traces of roads and streets, and the recent construction of ad hoc ammunition and supply facilities near the wharf resurrected by Confederate authorities using the ghost town as a base of operations, only the hulking shells of a few empty, decaying structures provided any clue as to Blakeley's former activity. "Blakeley," in the words of one observer sent to report on the grand federal military campaign aimed at the capture of Mobile, the last major Southern city to remain in Confederate hands in 1865, was really "no place at all."[1]

Yet the place remained a landmark for a region that had witnessed relatively slow overall pace of development since its unexpected economic heyday back in the 1820s when its future seemed so bright. The name Blakeley still evoked a sense of place, even if the promise it once held seemed to have, like its former residents, moved on. Upriver and downriver from the tranquil bluffs on which the town of Blakeley had sprung like one of the many bubbling springs from its shady ravines lay a patchwork of small farms scattered along the web of regional paths connecting the Tensaw area to other places. There was scarcely another community consisting of more than a handful of family farms along its course, though, save for the crossroads town of Stockton near its banks along its northern reaches. Coming into its own in the late 1830s and growing slowly to perhaps a few hundred residents by the time of the Civil War, Stockton had its mail delivered via the river and shipped some of its cotton away on its waters. Corn and other subsistence crops were grown in abundance by hardy yeomen farmers throughout the river region, and residents dabbled in various other agricultural enterprises at different points during the antebellum era. Tensaw River region planter Origen Sibley, for example, had experimented in silk production in the 1840s, importing thousands of mulberry trees to provide a home for delicate silkworms, but that grand trial had very limited success. Save for the contextually small amount of cotton produced by enslaved laborers on the few true Old South plantations along the Tensaw corridor, so did others. The river region may have been located in the Deep South, but it was quite a distance away from the heart of cotton country in Alabama's famed Black Belt and Tennessee Valley and far indeed from the white-columned mansions and sprawling estates of those regions. In 1860 just a little over 7,000 people, white and Black combined, called Baldwin County home, and no major urban center on par with Blakeley's one-time rival of Mobile could be found anywhere within it. Mobile, though, realized in full the antebellum promise Josiah Blakeley had envisioned along the Tensaw. By 1860 it had become home to nearly 30,000 residents, a bustling center of trade, and the second largest port on the Gulf of Mexico behind only New Orleans. Its prominence would eventually make it a prime target for the federal army as the Civil War raged across the country between 1861 and 1865.

The war's direct impact on the Tensaw proved relatively slight over the course of its first three years. Local residents followed its progress generally in much the same fashion as residents of many

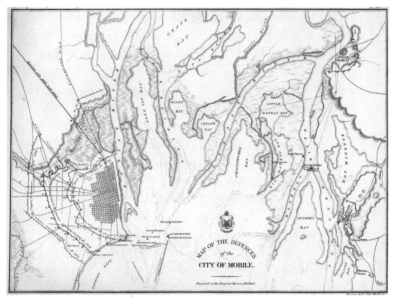

Map of defenses in the Mobile area during the Civil War. Courtesy of the Library of Congress.

other regions did. They monitored the results of the campaigning in newspapers; they kept track of family members and friends on faraway battlefields through letters; they noted the comings and goings of blockade runners, which successfully navigated their way through the porous blockade and into Mobile's harbor; and they dealt with occasional shortages of or price hikes on various items much easier to come by before the war. Unique to the Delta region, however, they observed with interest the creation of the various defenses along regional waterways to guard against an enemy approach to Mobile. The city itself lay ringed by fortifications, and the rivers and bay surrounding it were laced with gun emplacements, pilings restricting access to navigable channels, and even underwater mines. Any campaigning to capture Mobile would require a large combined-forces operation, and the longer the city avoided coming into the crosshairs of the Union army and navy the larger those numbers of men and material required to capture it became. As the war's fourth summer entered its longest sweltering days, the eventuality seemed as remote as ever.

Mobile's role, and by extension the Tensaw's, in the war began a dramatic change on the morning of August 5, 1864, when Admiral David G. Farragut sailed his fleet of warships into Mobile Bay from the open waters of the Gulf. Braving the numerous large-caliber artillery pieces of Fort Morgan, a channel full of deadly mines, and a small but potent Confederate naval squadron, by the end of the day the federal navy had established control of the bay and ended Mobile's days as a blockade-running port by effectively cutting the city off from the Gulf. Yet the city remained in rebel hands, one of the South's last major Confederate-controlled urban centers. Farragut steamed up to the city's outer defenses on the heels of his success in the lower bay to see if it might be within his power to change that situation, but he backed away convinced, as he put it in homespun fashion, the city would be "an elephant and take a large army to hold it." Neither the federal army or navy was quite prepared for said pachyderm at that moment, but the day in which they would was not long in coming. The federal high command had considered attempting the capture of Mobile as early as 1862, but the project was delayed repeatedly as other pressing military objectives demanded attention. In the spring of 1865, though, General Ulysses S. Grant finally assigned General Edward S. Canby for the task. Canby would ultimately have at his disposal some 45,000 men for the job and be assisted by a naval flotilla of over thirty warships under the command of Admiral Henry Knox Thatcher. Should the capture of Mobile be deemed impractical at the moment, Grant advised, Canby was to ascend the Delta and move on Selma and Montgomery, leaving Mobile isolated and useless to what remained of the rebellion.

Canby realized any attempt to attack Mobile head-on would be a fool's errand, but he could not make himself entirely comfortable with the idea of bypassing the long-sought city as he pursued other targets inland for reasons political and logistical. Studying regional maps, he quickly determined gaining control of the Tensaw to be necessary regardless of either course he pursued, and he set that goal as paramount. The problem lay in the fact that the Confederates anticipated the same course of action for any prospective enemy attacker and had been hard at work building a network of defenses along the Delta's eastern shores almost since the final shots of the Battle of Mobile Bay. As the federal forces assembled for the advance into the Delta region from the choppy waters of the entrance to Mobile Bay and from the breezy shores of Pensacola Bay, a showdown loomed.

The meeting place would be an impressive series of fortifications on the Delta's eastern shores built by the grueling labor of impressed workers and Confederate troops. Along the high bluffs overlooking the Apalachee River where stood a fortification long rumored to date to the Spanish colonial period, they had built an interconnected ring of earthworks that became known as Spanish Fort. At the time of the arrival of Union forces, it would be garrisoned by 2,500 or so of the roughly 9,000 men department commander General Dabney H. Maury had at his disposal for the defense of the Mobile area. Just upriver, at the junction of the deep and wide Apalachee and Blakeley Rivers, stood two artillery batteries—known as Huger and Tracy—rising from the Delta marsh on engineered earthen platforms that protected access to the Tensaw.

A short distance upstream along the immutable Tensaw lay the largest defensive post of them all. Fort Blakeley, as it was known, featured some three miles of interconnected earthen fortifications arranged in a broad arc around the site of the town of Blakeley, its northern and southern ends anchored on the shimmering river. In front of this Confederate line virtually all of the trees had been cut down for several hundred yards. Fort Blakeley's defenders meant this open ground to serve as a field of fire. Not only would anyone daring approach come within range of rebel guns, but all manner of other obstructions placed in the opening defied easy approach. The timber felled to create these fields of fire lay strewn across the expansive void between the tree line and the Confederate parapet. A few hundred yards out from the lines in several locations were minefields where "subterra shells" had been hidden in the ground, awaiting only the trod of a soldier to do their deadly work. Closer in were rows of abatis formed from the tops of felled trees; negotiating this tangle of debris on foot while under fire promised to be a hazardous duty. Rows of substantial rifle pits, where squads of skirmishers could be placed as an around-the-clock alarm system and first line of defense, guarded against surprise attack and added another layer of danger to any planned assault. The rebels had also stealthily strung telegraph wire between stumps of some of the trees that had been cut down to serve as an unexpected trip hazard. Beyond all this, just a few dozen yards from the main line in front of the redoubts, or miniforts where artillery and troops were concentrated, were rows of sharpened stakes with ominous points bristling defiance to intruders. Finally, a deep and wide dry ditch fronted the redoubts, which would force any troops somehow

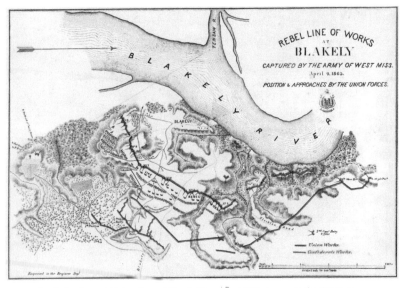

Confederate and Union lines at the Battle of Fort Blakeley; note the Tensaw is mislabeled as the "Blakeley" River. Courtesy of the Library of Congress.

successfully making their way to the main line to scale the steep slope of the fortification before gaining entry.

Louisiana planter St. John Richardson Liddell held overall command at Blakeley, leading just over 3,500 men possessing the extremes on the spectrum of combat experience. About half were serving their fourth year in Confederate gray, having enlisted early in the war and endured siege and privation at Vicksburg, confronted one of the largest federal armies to be put into the field in the western theater at several pitched battles in front of Atlanta and remained steady through bitter cold to fight overwhelming numbers on the frosty fields at Nashville. The other half of Blakeley's defenders were raw teenage conscripts and a sprinkling of men in their late forties or early fifties who had been too old for previous drafts and for whom the coming siege would be their first taste of combat. Such was the ragtag force that aimed to transform the arcing complex of earthworks on the Tensaw into the literal last ditch defending Mobile.

On April 1, 1865, federal columns began arriving at the outskirts of Blakeley. Ultimately some 16,000 troops would lay siege to the place and construct a concentric series of earthworks dug by hand and under fire in the attempt to strangle the Confederate stronghold. Hardy midwestern veterans, a smattering of men from states of the East Coast, and, notably, nearly 5,000 African American soldiers comprised their ranks. Progressively closer to Fort Blakeley, through ravines, swamps, dense brush, and open longleaf pine savannas, they crept throughout the first week of April. In near round-the-clock fighting featuring exchanges of small arms by skirmishers as well as artillery, they did their best to add Blakeley to the growing list of Confederate catastrophes that month, which collectively brought to an end the bitter four-year struggle for an independent Southern nation.

It was deadly work, each day's progress marked by mounting casualties and loss of life. The Confederates did what they could to make it as treacherous as possible by mounting surprise small-scale attacks and lighting up the nighttime sky under which the Yankees feverishly labored to advance their earthworks with calcium light flares that exposed, however briefly, troop dispositions. The noise of all the activity rising from the battlefield thundered across the waters of the Delta into Mobile and throughout the bay region for miles. By the end of the siege, the battlefield at Fort Blakeley looked and felt more like the contested terrain of Europe in the calamity known as World War I than anything most of the soldiers there had conceived when the war began—a complicated network of opposing trenches and a no-man's-land standing between.

This was a true combined-forces operation, and during the siege the river itself witnessed its share of maneuvering by the vessels of the Union and Confederate navies on its glistening waters. No fewer than nine federal vessels would be lost south of Blakeley during the campaign, most the victims of floating mines Confederate engineers had laced throughout the waterways in an attempt to restrict their enemy's ability to move upriver and rain artillery fire on the rebel lines. On the Tensaw behind Fort Blakeley the ships of the small Confederate squadron under Commander Ebenezer Farrand attempted to slow the advance of the federal army by lobbing shells of their own. The sidewheel steamer CSS *Morgan*, a survivor of the Battle of Mobile Bay, and the CSS *Nashville*, one of the largest ironclads built by the Confederacy, did what they could to make life uncomfortable for the bluecoats before guns could be put into place to drive them off.

A week into the siege the measured pace of the deadly dance playing out on the Tensaw suddenly picked up tempo. On the evening of April 8, the garrison downriver at Spanish Fort, having endured a nearly two-week-long harrowing siege against a force a dozen times its size, was at last compelled to abandon that post in a desperate bid to avoid capture. Canby's men gained what they felt was a hollow victory when on the morning of Sunday, April 9, 1865, sunrise revealed Spanish Fort in their possession but its army vanished. They would take pains to avoid a similar result at Fort Blakeley. The movement of transport vessels to and from the Blakeley dock, where they came to pick up a few evacuees from Spanish Fort who had made their way through the swamp during the night, only heightened fears that Fort Blakeley might be summarily abandoned. By midmorning, plans for an immediate assault were underway. The appointed time was 5:30 p.m.

With the exception of artillery and a few reserve units, virtually the entire besieging army stepped into motion by a quarter to six that evening, a massive wave of thousands of blue-clad troops forming a thick, undulating, line snaking across the broken landscape as men made a pell-mell advance toward the Confederate position. The clatter of small-arms fire and the thunderous report of shell bursts soon rose above the field of battle, interspersed by the shrill timbre of yells from scores of attackers, while the fluttering flags representing infantry and artillery units hailing from nearly twenty states pierced the smoky haze engulfing the scene. For an

The Last Stand for Mobile, by Rick Reeves. Courtesy of Historic Blakeley State Park and the Baldwin County Commission.

Depiction of the Battle of Fort Blakeley that appeared in *Harper's Weekly* shortly after the battle. Courtesy of the Library of Congress.

interminable few moments of terrible grandeur, the plains and ravines bordering the Tensaw stood witness to one of the grandest
spectacles of the Civil War. "We had a good view," remembered
one Yankee artillerist. "It was a glorious sight, a line of 15,000 men
marching steady into the jaws of death."[2]

On the ground, in the heart of the maelstrom, the attack was
less fantastic tapestry and more of a brutal and disorienting episode filled with peril. The attackers had barely emerged from their
trenches when explosions of black smoke and earth could be seen
shooting upward in isolated places as portions of the Yankee force
stepped into fields strewn with land mines. The deadly devices sev-
ered legs and arms from bodies and ripped through flesh and bone
with brutal suddenness. In another instant, the full weight of rebel
ordnance along Fort Blakeley's ramparts was being directed at the
attackers—hundreds of rifles sending heavy lead bullets whizzing
downrange and artillery of a variety of calibers in flaming bellows
launching hundreds of pounds of grapeshot, canister, solid shot,
and shell howling into the mass of humanity. The battlefield at once
became, observed one survivor of the attack, an immense "awful
hissing seething roaring fire of flame." The heavy cloud of sulfu-
rous smoke from the discharge of all the combined weaponry soon
hung heavy in the spring air, seemingly hastening dusk.[3]

Once the Union columns made it to the main lines of the fort,
a series of brief, close-quarters firefights erupted all along its length.
Nine individual battles in miniature raged around each of the nine
redoubts of Fort Blakeley for a few frenzied minutes, each marked
with acts of remarkable bravery amid the whirlwind of violence and
confusion. One by one, each bastion fell as it was overwhelmed,

The CSS *Nashville*, which was operating on the Tensaw at the time of the Battle of Fort Blakeley. Courtesy of the Alabama Department of Archives and History, Montgomery.

and its defenders alternately fled rearward or laterally or stood to make a bold last stand where they were. Hundreds fell before the rattle of musketry eventually slowed to the point individual pops became discernible, and singular voices from the throats of the contending combatants could be heard. The last shots were fired along and into the Tensaw itself, where a few hundred rebels attempted a frantic escape via the watery corridor to Mobile aboard planks hastily ripped from docks. A few managed to hop aboard the CSS *Nashville* as it shoved off into the river's current, some of the few dozen to avoid capture in the last gasp for Confederate hopes in the Gulf region. By 6:15 p.m., the entire fight drew to a close up and down the Blakeley line, and a resounding, rolling, cheer went up along its length from the victors. An eerie silence followed as the acrid smell of smoke hung thick in the humid Delta air.

The next day all the artillery that could be brought to bear began a bombardment of the island fortifications of Huger and Tracy—the only Confederate positions still standing between Mobile and the federal forces. The affair proved brief. Realizing their predicament, the defenders of these posts evacuated on April 11. On April 12 federal officers received the surrender of the long-sought city without another shot being fired, the remnants of Maury's tattered force having fled upriver slightly ahead of them.

Aerial view of the battlefield at Blakeley, showing the area of Redoubt 4 with the Tensaw River in the background. Photograph by Fort Rucker Warrant Officer Candidate School, Courtesy of Historic Blakeley State Park.

It just delayed the inevitable. The Mobile area, and virtually every militarily significant point in the state, lay under federal control by that point. In May the last formal surrender of Rebel troops east of the Mississippi occurred just outside of Mobile and involved some of the men who had so recently been pledged to its defense. By that time a new era had already begun along the Tensaw.

6

~~~

For Work and Play

The Tensaw flowed on after the guns of the Civil War fell silent, as unaffected by the episode in the cataclysmic conflict that had just played out along its banks as the accomplishments and failures of the natives of ancient times. But much as the river rolled through the ensuing decades little changed, in a way so did the larger basin that is so connected with its waters. To suggest the century after the war was a period of stability along the Tensaw's shores is at best an oversimplification of regional history, which glosses over a host of groundbreaking cultural change and technological developments. But as far as the regional population's interaction with the age-old stream went, the postwar decades were characterized much more by constancy than mutability, by steadiness than upheaval. Small, isolated private farmsteads, commercial timber harvesting, and subsistence fishing persisted up and down the river's reaches during this interlude. The era featured less of the drama-filled epics of community-building, international intrigue, and martial pageant, which so easily yield themselves to legend, and more of the humdrum but elemental tale of human interface with the environment.

And so the river coursed throughout the remainder of the nineteenth century and into the twentieth, a vital if unheralded lifeline to hundreds of people who drew sustenance from its waters and the lush lowlands it drained. Those residing alongside the Tensaw angled its waters for catfish, bream, bass, speckled trout, redfish, sheepshead, and mullet. They even stalked frogs and alligators and all manner of other edible aquatic creatures. They farmed its cleared patches of grassy areas, growing corn and cotton and small plots of peas, beans, and a number of other vegetables, and they grazed their cattle on the bottomlands enriched by the river's periodic inundations, especially Delta islands that served as natural pens. They hunted for the meat and pelts of forest-dwelling creatures that called the river region home—deer, squirrel, rabbits, and other game—and swung their shotguns toward the sky to attempt to bag the swift-winged ducks flying along the river's course.

Logging proved to be by far the largest agricultural enterprise undertaken in a coordinated fashion in the upper Delta for the better part of a century. Throughout the latter decades of the nineteenth century and up to approximately the halfway point of the twentieth, timber assumed a position as the primary resource being extracted from the swampy floodplains through which the Tensaw charted its meandering course. Generations of loggers helped supply the insatiable demand for timber throughout the growing nation and beyond by the harvest of enormous numbers of trees. Virgin stands of cypress, oak, ash, cottonwood, tupelo, sycamore, hackberry, and others were felled during an era of dramatic deforestation that altered the very appearance of the region through which the mighty Tensaw cut. Evidence of logging activity can be found along the river's shores and throughout the region still to-day in the forms of scars on the land of various forms. The most obvious, though, is the conspicuous absence of truly massive trees, some of the largest of their species that had stood witness to the river's inexorable flow. The legendary former State Champion Bald Cypress, likely left standing due to damage sustained from a long-ago lightning strike, its inaccessible location, or both, provides a hint of what once towered over the Tensaw.

The sojourn of timber men on the Tensaw is one of the more colorful tales associated with this period. These workers were

Logging has always been labor-intensive work. This crew, believed to be working in southern Clarke County just north of the Tensaw, is shown in a scene typical of the time and region. They are using horses, oxen, and man-power to maneuver logs, each weighing thousands of pounds, out of the forest. Courtesy of the Doy Leale McCall Rare Book and Manuscript Library, University of South Alabama.

Logs being prepared for shipment at the port of Mobile. Courtesy of the Doy Leale McCall Rare Book and Manuscript Library, University of South Alabama.

sturdy and tough, but they needed more than sheer brawn to be successful. They had to have an intricate knowledge of trees and the environments in which they grew to perform their jobs, and by extension, simply to stay alive. Harvesting lumber required scouting out areas that would yield the most return per day of labor ahead of time, a consideration imbued with special significance given that the work often had to be carefully timed to occur during the relatively short periods of dry weather prior to predictable periods of high water in the Delta. This meant that trees must be felled at specific times ahead of the floods so that they could be floated out of the swamp before they rotted or would potentially sink to the bottom of the murky water during their passage. May and October tended to be drier months, with high water usually arriving in late fall and early spring, and work was planned accordingly. But in addition to a familiarity with natural cycles, it took a special skill borne only through firsthand experience on the business end of an ax or whipsaw to be able to make a tree fall exactly where one wanted. Deadly "widow-makers" and kicking butt ends could be lethal if one was not careful about his task and planned out exactly what he wanted to have happen before sawing into a tree. No matter how the job was done, it necessitated taxing manual labor reserved for only the hardiest of souls.

Different circumstances called for different methods of getting the lumber to market, all of them as labor intensive as felling the trees. The most elemental, although it was by no means simple, relied on rising water to do much of the heavy lifting. After timber in a selected tract had been felled, the logs could be floated out of the swamp and into the river for the long journey to mills and other processing centers and the docks of Mobile. Like any enterprise requiring skilled labor, this proved much more difficult than it sounds. Even the seemingly straightforward process of floating logs out of the swamp and to the main river channel demanded complicated preparatory work in devising a series of makeshift dams and small-scale canals to ensure water levels were high enough to be able to reliably transport the cargo.

The haul was bound together in one of several types of rafts of varying shape and size and guided from the Delta swamp and down the Tensaw by skilled laborers known simply as watermen. Down the river these gangly, transient watercraft composed of logs went, with the adroit watermen, legendary in their knowledge of the waterway, guiding them from perilous perches atop the slippery logs. The whole scene conjures up something from a storybook about the Wild West—man and the natural environment both larger than life engaged in rollicking, superhuman adventure. It is an era and an occupation sadly almost entirely lost to lore, as few have attempted to chronicle the exploits of the workers who brought the bounty of the Tensaw swamps to market. One outstanding account is Robert Leslie Smith's reminiscences of logging and rafting in the Delta, *Gone to the Swamp*. Smith's unique and authoritative account of life along the Tensaw and the larger Delta celebrates the loggers and their equipment with a flare only a veteran of their noisy streamside worksites and roaring campfire-lit wilderness bases could provide. It is an ode to a way of life that experienced its heyday in the early twentieth century but had practically disappeared by the 1950s.[1]

Less flamboyant but just as intense were more traditional methods of timber harvesting. Using oxen and large-wheeled carts—and later, trucks and other mechanized equipment—supplemented by copious doses of manpower, workers toiled in muddy slop to haul enormous logs weighing thousands of pounds each out of the swampy bottoms where they could be transported to market. Short, temporary rail lines laid for that exclusive purpose sometimes provided a critical interim link in moving the harvest along its way. In many places they served as a smaller-scale conveyance to the larger locomotives that would haul tons of raw lumber along regional railways to area sawmills. Tracts adjacent to

A clearcut section of Delta lands. Helicopters have been used to haul out logs from cuttings such as this in recent decades. Courtesy of the Doy Leale McCall Rare Book and Manuscript Library, University of South Alabama.

the river itself could be much more effectively logged by the use of pullboats. Essentially a large winch on a barge, these workhorse machines, at first steam-powered and later driven by internal combustion engines, were used to drag logs from where they lay to the river using cables and chains. The deep trenches and furrows left by their work are in places still visible. It was quite literally tough sledding for all involved, regardless of the method engaged.

But other products from the Tensaw region's vast stands of timber required the trees to stay in place and very much alive. The hardwoods of the swampy bottoms may have been prized for their durable lumber, but the endless tracts of nearby upland longleaf and slash pine yielded a variety of products from their resin by the barrel. It was a slow and labor-intensive process, requiring slashing of the trees so the slow-moving liquid could drain into collection cups before harvesting, but it employed workers by the hundreds in the collection of millions of barrels of the stuff over the course of decades of production. In the days of wooden ships in the colonial and early American periods pine species had become an invaluable source of the pitch and tar used to caulk seams between hull planks, but the distillation of turpentine from resin for use as a solvent and in a variety of applications ranging from medicine to soap and varnish assumed a position as a leading regional industry by the late 1800s. It would remain so until about the time major timber harvesting began to play out in the 1950s, once the most productive stands had been cut down, causing an abrupt abandonment of a way of life and business that had been associated with the Tensaw for the better part of a century. Harvesting of timber of course continues even to this day in the region drained by the river, but it is more targeted, much more mechanized, and an altogether different enterprise from the days of the watermen or the turpentine collectors.

The small volume of commercial traffic on the Tensaw, miniscule compared to that of the burgeoning waterway across the Delta servicing the steadily growing port of Mobile, declined as the nineteenth century gave way to the twentieth. There was, for a time, however, some considerable if infrequent ferry traffic on the river as steamboats connected the terminus of the Mobile and Great Northern Railroad—at Tensaw Station (Hurricane

Landing)—with Mobile. The M&GN was essentially a sixty-seven mile spur, connecting to the main line of the Alabama and Florida Railroad. A bridge to complete the route had been desired by the railway's operators from the time of its planning in the 1850s, but one would not be constructed over the Delta until the 1920s.

In contrast to the boom in commercial activity witnessed at the shipyards and docks in Mobile during the world wars era, a quiet type of equilibrium prevailed up and down the tranquil Tensaw. By the mid-twentieth century the river had come full circle through upheavals foreign and domestic to resume its condition as a wild, free-flowing natural habitat only sporadically disturbed by the chug of boat engines. When, not long after the end of World War II, the federal government determined to store hundreds of mothballed oceangoing merchant ships in the waters of the Mobile area as part of the National Defense Reserve Fleet, the sleepy river became a ready-made maritime warehouse whose usage would minimally interfere with commercial navigation. Beginning in 1947 and continuing through the early 1970s the Mobile Reserve Fleet lay at anchor in neat rows along a stretch of the Tensaw just north of the site of the old town of Blakeley. The ships were kept in readiness to be pressed into service in short notice in case of national emergency by a small force of workers who went from ship to ship checking mechanical equipment and briefly firing engines. Remembered by the ominous-sounding name of the "Ghost Fleet," these mothballed ships formed a unique and memorable sort of floating landmark whose site, according to the many witnesses to the scene still living in the river region, was truly something to behold. Over 800 vessels, mostly decommissioned Liberty or Victory ships, were ultimately moored in the Tensaw at some point, a few hundred at any given time being stationed there and hundreds of others moved in or out during given years. The ships were brought into the moorage through a canal dredged through the channel of a small creek flowing between the Mobile and the Tensaw especially

Towing Reserve Fleet ships upriver, ca. 1950. *Mobile Press Register* Collection, the Doy Leale McCall Rare Book and Manuscript Library, University of South Alabama.

(Right) Ships of the "Ghost Fleet" at anchor. Courtesy of United States Department of Transportation, Maritime Administration Division.

Remains of docks built for servicing reserve fleet ships near Hurricane Landing. Courtesy of Mike Bunn.

for the purpose. The spoil was piled in heaps along the route, the most prominent being a deposit of sand that forms the peculiar beach on the northern end of Gravine Island. The last of the vessels were removed in 1973. Aside from a few old pilings and the submerged wreckage of a handful of ship hulls used to form artificial reefs in the Gulf of Mexico, only their memory remains.

Outside of the few commercial fishermen operating primarily at the mouth of the river in pursuit of shrimp, crabs, and other aquatic species in demand by area bait shops and restaurants, today the only regular river traffic on the Tensaw is purely recreational. Hobby and tournament fishermen, kayakers, and captains of guided sightseeing cruises aboard multipassenger pontoon boats are usually the only navigators plying the full reach of the Tensaw's sweeping curves. Seeking spots to while away the time trying to catch a mess of fish for the fryer, trying to tip the scales for the end-of-day weigh-in, or otherwise engaged in voyages of discovery to connect with its storied past or individually commune with its lush natural habitat, these sojourners form the core of the river's visitorship. Depending on the season, birdwatchers and waterborne duck hunters use the river as well as they travel to the best spots for their particular diversions.

The natural abundance and splendid isolation afforded on and along the Tensaw's waters has always attracted the type of enthusiast who savors the chance to get away from the rest of civilization. Today it continues to do so, and those full- and part-time residents are a special part of the region's mystique as a place apart. In recent years novelist Watt Key famously introduced readers everywhere to the Delta's "Swamp People," shedding light on the colorful personalities and the special community of those who appreciate and love the region and are willing to endure the tribulations that come with spending time on the Tensaw and its neighboring streams.

The Tensaw at Cliff's Landing, site of a moorage for reserve fleet ships.
Courtesy of Mike Bunn.

Cruise up the river a short distance north of Interstate 65 and one will find dozens of houseboats lining the river's banks near Lower Bryant Landing, some occupied seasonally by fishers but a few near-permanent residences (at least until high waters force even these hardy souls to seek higher ground). Spaced out in scattered intervals to the north and south of the landing are other perma-nent cabins used as vacation retreats by a small number of families

who retain title to various plots predating the era of public ownership of much of the Delta's trackless acreage. Built on stilts and accessed only by boat, these cottages are of varying sophistication, but even the smallest required Herculean effort to construct and only slightly less so to maintain—they are enduring testimony to the power of the draw of the river on those blessed with the opportunity to spend time along its shores and the lengths they are willing to go to in order to experience its grandeur. A few hunting camps along the river's northern reaches, one in continuous operation since the late 1940s, still serve as the spot for weekend recreation among small groups of hunters and fishermen seeking outdoor adventure within a short drive of home. All along the river's small bluffs and swampy shores, deer and hog hunters still stalk their prey in fall and winter. Once virtually eliminated from the forests of the area, deer have made a remarkable comeback thanks to concerted regional wildlife management programs. So have

Tensaw River Hunting Club along the upper reaches of the Tensaw. Courtesy of Mike Bunn.

other species hunted almost to extinction in the past but now some of the Tensaw region's most famous modern-day occupants—alligators and black bears.[2]

The fact that so much of the region through which the Tensaw flows is publicly owned has had a lot to do with both the health of its wildlife population and its continuing undeveloped condition. The US Army Corps of Engineers had acquired several large tracts of thousands of acres of lower Delta lands by the 1980s, in the process helping ensure it would remain in a wild state for coming generations. Beginning in the 1990s, the state of Alabama also became a major player in regional land ownership through the activities of the Forever Wild Land Trust. Under the provisions of a bill passed in 1992 and reaffirmed on its scheduled sunset in 2012, both by remarkably large margins of Alabama voters, the trust has been able to acquire and protect hundreds of thousands of acres of wildlands across the state. In the Mobile-Tensaw Delta alone, the trust now owns nearly 50,000 acres of land. Many of these purchases were made possible by the fortuitous fact that wetlands are not particularly well-suited to development and thus are often available for acquisition at somewhat modest prices. How keen is the irony that some of the most pivotal acreage to regional habitat health is some of the most affordable? The Delta's unique natural diversity and the fact that nearly half of its acreage is already publicly owned has led some to occasionally question whether the region might be offered to the federal government for management as a national park. It is an intriguing concept but one fraught with problems by the score—financial, political, philosophical—and for those reasons and more the issue seems for the moment to have been decided solidly in favor of the status quo. Whatever its future, the Delta's rich natural and cultural heritage are sure to play a prominent part in regional culture and in providing the backdrop for its unique sense of place.

Afterword

R IVERS ARE AT THEIR HEART LIFE-GIVERS, EXISTING SYMBI-
otically with the life they support whether that be in the most
basic items of sustenance or as the platform for financial transac-
tions conducted for the purchase of an experience. Although extraction of resources from waterways and alterations in their natural flow are pursuits especially rife with opportunities for abuse in
our contemporary times, there seems comparatively little reason
to fear the Tensaw is in danger of any particular looming physical
catastrophe any more treacherous than those threatening other regional waterways. Admittedly, its flow has been altered to some degree by upstream dams, and we are only beginning to understand
the effects of such changes on wildlife habitat, much less the larger
concerns associated with global climate change. Pollution is always
a problem given the interconnected nature of our streams and the
enormous amounts of contaminants being dumped or washed into
them. Plus, all these are issues that current laws seem inadequate to
address sufficiently. Yet the situation could be worse.

There is almost no recent industrial development along the
Tensaw's course, and the modest pace of domestic construction

along its banks would appear sustainable with responsible regulation. There is no ongoing dredging, no plans for damming the river's waters, and relatively little commercial fishing that might either alter the river's flow or severely threaten any certain species. One need only look at the mighty river's mouth to see the slow-building but cumulative effects of the millions of tons of silt carried along the Tensaw and other Delta waters in the form of shallow, grassless bays with severely diminished aquatic life and less migratory bird species to understand what alteration of natural cycles can do. Statistics bear out that extinction is a general threat across the board in the state's rivers, the Tensaw being no exception. Alabama is rightfully proud of its position as the leader in the nation's aquatic species diversity, but on the other side of that coin is the ugly truth that at least owing in part to the fact it is home to so many, it also ranks at the top of documented extinctions. But these problems are broader than the river's lone reach, and the stream seems to have been spared some of the worst effects of mankind's heedless manipulation. Even though the Tensaw and the life it sustains have, in short, been severely affected by human activity, owing to its somewhat undeveloped location and the corresponding "benign neglect" journalist and author Ben Raines notes it has endured for well over a century, it is healthier than we might otherwise have reason to expect.[1]

We sometimes need to be reminded, too, that river systems are dynamic, living, ecosystems that experience some change over time even in the best of circumstances. Our interference has sped up the pace of change in harmful ways and disrupted ancient cycles all over the planet in recent times, to be sure, but over the long arc

Historic Blakeley State Park's *Delta Explorer* on a Tensaw River cruise. Photography by SkyBama, courtesy of Historic Blakeley State Park.

of thousands of years dramatic changes to the natural environment manifest themselves that are a normal part of life across the globe. The attempt to respect and preserve a natural environment does not necessarily mean we can ensure it stays in exactly the same condition forever, but rather that it experiences change more naturally.

In summary, at the time of this writing, the Tensaw would appear ideally positioned to continue to serve in its ancient role as lifeblood of a distinct geographical, natural, and cultural region despite all the concerns confronting its health. Responsible

Fishing tournament at Live Oak Landing. Photography by Kristina Pittman, courtesy of the North Baldwin Chamber of Commerce.

stewardship is, of course, key. That human enjoyment of the river's essence and the life it currently and has in the past sustained—recreational and heritage tourism for lack of a better term—seems to be a promising part of the future for the Tensaw augers well for mankind's relationship with the mighty stream. The river, as we have seen, has much to offer for the edification and education of locals and visitors alike, and such use is not only sustainable but potentially financially lucrative. The river corridor is a long way from having the infrastructure to support its becoming a true national ecotourism destination, but access is easy enough for the number of current users and there is no reason to think it could not grow commensurate with additional traffic in the future. Historic Blakeley State Park's *Delta Explorer* already plies the river's waters on guided cruises showcasing its rich heritage year-round, and several smaller cruising outfits also guide adventurers in discovery of its watery wonders. The numerous small landings in varied states of development spaced out along the eastern banks of its winding route allow boaters safe and convenient points of entry independent of any guided touring. It goes almost without saying that there is much to be desired in stewardship of the larger region through which the Tensaw pursues its course to Mobile Bay, and there is much room for improvement on any number of fronts as it concerns oversight, access, and education. But one could argue that, all things considered, our inheritance of this natural wonder could come with far more vexations.

The Tensaw still flows free and bountiful, sparking the imagination of those with an awareness of the human history that has played out along its shores for millennia. It is an exceptional and unrecognized heritage corridor worthy of celebration and awaiting discoverers. If the river's past reveals anything about its future, it demonstrates the likelihood for continued change in how humans interact with it. Whether the Tensaw becomes a tourist destination, a natural preserve, or even at some distant point a population center, the river will roll on, its waters carrying past and future stories both mundane and transcendent to Mobile Bay.

(Right) Rainbow over the Tensaw. Courtesy of Sherry Stimpson Frost.

Notes

Chapter 1

1. Gregory A. Waselkov, C. Fred Andrus, and Glenn E. Plumb, eds., *A State of Knowledge of the Natural, Cultural, and Economic Resources of the Greater Mobile-Tensaw River Area* (Fort Collins, CO: National Park Service, 2016), xix.

Chapter 2

1. Richebourg Gaillard McWilliams, ed., *Iberville's Gulf Journals* (Tuscaloosa: University of Alabama Press, 1981), 168. Investigation into Mound L on the Bottle Creek site has revealed evidence that someone was apparently still living there in the early eighteenth century but not utilizing readily-available European items as were so many of their neighbors. Whether this occupation was in some way related to the site's ritual significance or not is unknown. See Ian W. Brown, ed., *Bottle Creek: A Pensacola Culture Site in South Alabama* (Tuscaloosa: University of Alabama Press, 2003), 94, 109.

Chapter 3

1. The quote about Mobile's unhealthiness is taken from copies of original papers found in the British Colonial Office Records, microfilmed copies of which are available at the University of West Florida. It was brought to light to historians of the era in an article by Dr. Robert R. Rea titled "Graveyard for Britons," West Florida, 1763–1781," *Florida Historical*

Quarterly 47, no. 4 (April 1969), 345–64. Bartram's quotes are taken from William Bartram, *Travels through North and South Carolina, Georgia, East and West Florida* (Philadelphia: James and Johnson, 1791), 404, 405.

Chapter 4

1. An unpublished account of the Byrne affair is found in the Albert James Pickett Papers, Alabama Department of Archives and History. Pickett was the author of *History of Alabama and Incidentally of Georgia and Mississippi from the Earliest Times* (Charleston: Walker and James, 1851), generally considered to be the first serious history of the state. His notes on the incident recounted here were taken from an interview with Gerald Byrne's son.

2. *St. Stephens Halcyon*, February 22, 1819.

3. Mary Y. Grice, "The Dead City of Blakeley," unpublished manuscript, Historic Blakeley State Park.

Chapter 5

1. Benjamin C. Truman, "The Campaign in Alabama," *New York Times*, April 24, 1865.

2. Henry W. Hart Letters, April 10, 1865, Special Collections, Virginia Polytechnic Institute and State University.

3. Hart Letters, April 10, 1865.

Chapter 6

1. Robert Leslie Smith, *Gone to the Swamp: Raw Materials for the Good Life in the Mobile-Tensaw Delta* (Tuscaloosa: University of Alabama Press, 2008).

2. Watt Key, *Among the Swamp People: Life in Alabama's Mobile-Tensaw River Delta* (Tuscaloosa: University of Alabama Press, 2015).

Afterword

1. The quote is taken from Ben Raines, *Saving America's Amazon: The Threat to Our Nation's Most Biodiverse River System* (Montgomery: NewSouth Books, 2020), 16.

Further Readings

THIS BOOK DRAWS ON A WIDE RANGE OF SCHOLARSHIP with diverse focuses to provide an introduction to an understudied region. Listed here are the primary sources consulted in its compilation. Taken together, they represent an essential reading list for any investigation into the river's history.

There are no book-length studies of the Tensaw as a distinct waterway itself. Rather, its history and natural environment are most often discussed in studies of the larger Mobile-Tensaw Delta region of which it is a part. One of the best overviews of the region's rich natural and cultural heritage is the study edited by Gregory A. Waselkov, C. Fred Andrus, and Glenn E. Plumb and published as part of a cooperative effort between the University of South Alabama, the University of Alabama, and the National Park Service. Titled *A State of Knowledge of the Natural, Cultural, and Economic Resources of the Greater Mobile-Tensaw River Area* (Fort Collins, CO: National Park Service, 2016), the publication is a comprehensive summary of what is known about the Delta's human history and abundant natural life. Some of the leading authorities in several areas of study were a part of the project. It is unquestionably the best single place to start for an understanding of the region.

The rich natural heritage of the Tensaw River and the larger Delta is discussed in numerous other books varying in scope from studies of Alabama's waterways in general to those investigating one particular species of its copious animal life. One of the best, and most unique, is *In the Realm of Rivers: Alabama's Mobile-Tensaw Delta* (Montgomery: NewSouth Books, 2005), by former state poet laureate Sue Walker and accomplished photographer Dennis Holt. An unconventional assemblage of ways to view and understand the Delta and its importance, the book features contributions by archaeologists, environmentalists, and others sharing a common interest and connection to this natural landmark to communicate its essence. Highlighting both the region's uniqueness and its fragility is Ben Raines's *Saving America's Amazon: The Threat to Our Nation's Most Biodiverse River System* (Montgomery: NewSouth, 2020). Raines's book is at once a thoughtful look at the abundance of life in Alabama's Mobile-Tensaw Delta and a warning about how endangered its environment stands. Other books useful in understanding the Tensaw as a unique natural habitat include *Alabama Rivers: A Celebration and Challenge*, by William G. Deutsch (Florence, AL: Mindbridge Press, 2019), which showcases the role of rivers in Alabama's past, present, and future. The book features lots of information on watershed formation, species diversification, habitat alteration, and pollution in each of Alabama's major river basins. But it also features some genuine attempts to mesh cultural heritage and the natural environment, making efforts to find the distinguishing features of the human history of each of the major river systems of Alabama from prehistoric times to the present. R. Scot Duncan's *Southern Wonder: Alabama's Surprising Biodiversity* (Tuscaloosa: University of Alabama Press, 2013) is an eye-opening celebration of the state's incredible diversity of wildlife and natural habitats and contains a concise summary of life in the Mobile-Tensaw Delta. Also useful is Doug Phillips and Robert P. Falls Sr.'s *Discovering Alabama Wetlands* (Tuscaloosa: University of Alabama Press, 2002). The multivolume series edited by Ralph E. Mirarchi and others, titled *Alabama Wildlife*, is perhaps the best single reference source on its subject.

For one of the most useful overviews of regional prehistory and the timeline of its ancient cultural development, see Judith Bense, *Archaeology of the Southeastern United States: Paleoindian to World War I* (San Diego: Academic Press, 1994). Any history of the Bottle Creek Mound Site begins with Ian W. Brown's remarkable volume of edited essays, *Bottle Creek: A Pensacola Culture Site in South Alabama* (Tuscaloosa: University of Alabama Press, 2003). The essential resource on this legendary Mississippian site, the book contains contributions by Brown and several other eminent archaeologists who have conducted research on the site and into the collections of materials retrieved from excavations there. As it stands as the only book-length professional study of the site, its importance to our understanding of it cannot be overstated. For brief summaries of the state of knowledge on the site, see Richard S. Fuller and Ian W. Brown, "The Mound Island Project: An Archaeological Survey in the Mobile-Tensaw Delta" (Alabama Museum of Natural History Bulletin No. 19) and Ian W. Brown, "Bottle Creek Site," Encyclopedia of Alabama, http://encyclopediaofalabama.org/article

/h-1160. Brown's *Bottle Creek Reflections: The Personal Side of Archaeology in the Mobile-Tensaw Delta* (Tuscaloosa: Borgo Publishing, 2012) is a journal of his experience conducting excavations at the site over multiple summers in the 1990s and contains some unique as-it-happened accounts of the discoveries the team made alongside chronicling the trials involved in the undertaking.

One of the oldest histories of the region is still among the most useful in the study of the Tensaw. Peter J. Hamilton's, *Colonial Mobile* (Boston: Houghton Mifflin, 1910) looms as a landmark in local historiography. While its focus is of course the city, it provides information on the full sweep of regional colonial heritage. For overviews of the French period in colonial history with a focus on the original settlement of Mobile, consult Jay Higginbotham's *Old Mobile: Fort de la Louisiane, 1702–1711* (Tuscaloosa: University of Alabama Press, 1991) and Gregory Waselkov's *Old Mobile Archaeology* (Tuscaloosa: University of Alabama Press, 1999). For a summary of some of the archaeological investigations into colonial-era plantation sites in the region, see Gregory A. Waselkov, Bonnie L. Gums, and Kristen J. Gremillion, *Plantation Archaeology at Rivière Aux Chiens, ca. 1725–1848* (Mobile: University of South Alabama Center for Archaeological Studies, 2000).

The history of the British period in Gulf Coast region has been chronicled in my book, *Fourteenth Colony: The Forgotten Story of the Gulf South during America's Revolutionary Era* (Montgomery: NewSouth Books, 2020). Any study of the Tensaw's colonial-era history must include William Bartram, *Travels through North and South Carolina, Georgia, East and West Florida* (Philadelphia: James and Johnson, 1791). For the troubled transition of the region to

American ownership from Spanish control, two of the most comprehensive and readable accounts are Robert V. Haynes, *The Mississippi Territory and the Southwest Frontier, 1795–1817* (Lexington: University Press of Kentucky, 2010) and Thomas D. Clark and John D. W. Guice, *The Old Southwest, 1795–1830: Frontiers in Conflict* (Norman: University of Oklahoma Press, 1996).

For general histories of Baldwin County and the Tensaw River region, see Kay Nuzum's *A History of Baldwin County* (Bay Minette, AL: Baldwin Times, 1971); O. Lawrence Burnette Jr.'s *Coastal Kingdom: A History of Baldwin County, Alabama* (Baltimore: PublishAmerica, 2006) and *Historic Baldwin County: A Bicentennial History* (San Antonio: Historical Publishing Network, 2007); and John C. Lewis and Harriet Brill Outlaw, *Images of America: Baldwin County* (Charleston: Arcadia Publishing, 2009). Older works include *A Brief History of Baldwin County* (Fairhope, AL: Baldwin County Historical Society, 1928), by L. J. Newcomb Comings, and Martha M. Albers and Prescott Parker's *Story of the Tensaw: Blakeley, Spanish Fort, Jackson Oaks, Fort Mims* (Montrose: P. A. Parker, 1922) is a brief volume containing some thirty-seven pages of text in the form of sentimental vignettes about local landmarks and the Battle of Fort Blakeley.

For a general overview of the territorial and early statehood years in Alabama, see Mike Bunn, *Early Alabama: An Illustrated Guide to the Formative Years, 1798–1826* (Tuscaloosa: University of Alabama Press, 2019). For summaries of the Tensaw region and the Creek War, see Gregory A. Waselkov's *A Conquering Spirit: Fort Mims and the Redstick War of 1813–1814* (Tuscaloosa: University of Alabama Press, 2006); *Battle for the Southern Frontier: The*

Creek War and the War of 1812 (Charleston: History Press, 2008) by Mike Bunn and Clay Williams; *A Paradise of Blood: The Creek War of 1813–1814* (Yardley, PA: Westholme, 2016) by Howard T. Weir III; and Peter Cozzen's *A Brutal Reckoning: Andrew Jackson, the Creek Indians, and the Epic War for the American South.*

A short, unpublished manuscript by Historic Blakeley State Park founder Mary Y. Grice titled "The Dead City of Blakeley," in the possession of the park, still stands among the best sources of information on the Tensaw's long-lost urban entity. See also "Blakeley" by Grant D. Hiatt, published as part of the online Encyclopedia of Alabama, http://encyclopediaofalabama.org/article/h-3023; James C. Parker, "Blakeley: A Frontier Seaport," *Alabama Review* 27 (January 1974): 39–51; and *Historic Blakeley State Park: A Guide to the History and Heritage* by Mike Bunn. For a history of the community of Stockton, see Lynn Hastie and Davida Richerson Hastie's The *Leaves of Stockton: A History of Stockton, Alabama* (Bay Minette, AL: Lavender Publishing, 2015).

There are plenty of resources on the Battle of Fort Blakeley and the larger Campaign for Mobile easily available. Despite the fight at Blakeley being one of the least-studied of any significant Civil War battle, as is so often the case with every aspect of that landmark conflict, a considerable body of literature nonetheless exists on the subject. The first comprehensive narrative on the campaign, Christopher C. Andrews, *History of the Campaign of Mobile* (New York: D. Van Nostrand, 1867), appeared just two years after the conclusion of the war. In more recent years, the long overlooked last major combined-forces affair has finally received the attention of scholars. Chester G. Hearn's *Mobile Bay and the*

Mobile Campaign: The Last Great Battles of the Civil War (Jefferson, NC: McFarland, 1998) is likely the most scholarly of them all, relying almost exclusively on primary resources to produce a detailed study of the entirety of the fighting between the Battle of Mobile Bay and the capture of the city of Mobile some nine months later. Sean Michael O'Brien's *Mobile, 1865: Last Stand of the Confederacy* (Westport, CT: Praeger, 2001) is a thorough account of the fighting around Spanish Fort and Blakeley focusing on the combat experience of the men in the ranks. Paul Brueske's *The Last Siege: The Mobile Campaign, Alabama 1865* (Oxford: Casemate, 2018) is a detailed but easily readable account of the campaign that brings to light a number of forgotten facts. My own account of the Battle of Fort Blakeley, *The Assault on Fort Blakeley: The Thunder and Lightning of Battle* (Charleston: History Press, 2021) is a brief summary and guide to the fighting drawing heavily on the reports and personal remembrances of its veterans.

There is precious little writing about logging, farming, and hunting in the Delta other than short anecdotal newspaper articles and oral legends. Robert Leslie Smith's *Gone to the Swamp: Raw Materials for the Good Life in the Mobile-Tensaw Delta* (Tuscaloosa: University of Alabama Press, 2008) is an incredible resource on a bygone and little-chronicled way of life in the region penned by one who knew it intimately. A Delta legend as enduring as any of the sites he documented, Smith published the book while in his nineties based on reflections of a lifetime of research and experience. The book gives some of the best detail on the techniques and strategies used by those who drew their living from the Tensaw region in the late nineteenth and early twentieth centuries. For a brief discussion of the origin of regional railroads, see *Railroads of the Confederacy* (Chapel Hill: University of North Carolina Press, 1952), by Robert C. Black III. Brief mentions of the Mobile Reserve Fleet in the Tensaw are found in several histories of the region, but few contain any more than the most cursory of information. The best single source of information is probably the "Mobile Reserve Fleet" subject file at the Doy Leale McCall Rare Book and Manuscript Library, University of South Alabama. For a general understanding of Alabama's Forever Wild program, see Doug Phillips, "Forever Wild Land Trust," Encyclopedia of Alabama, http://encyclopediaofalabama.org/article/h-1125. For a colorful account of the hardy and often eccentric characters who haunt the deep recesses of the Delta, see Watt Key, *Among the Swamp People: Life in Alabama's Mobile-Tensaw River Delta* (Tuscaloosa: University of Alabama Press, 2015).

Index